Gifts From The Poor

John F. Loya

WIPF & STOCK · Eugene, Oregon

Wipf and Stock Publishers
199 W 8th Ave, Suite 3
Eugene, OR 97401

Gifts from the Poor
By Loya, John F.

ISBN 13: 978-1-61097-556-8
Publication date 5/23/2011
Previously published by Winston-Derek Publishers, Inc., 1990

Dedicated to

Dorothy Kazel, O.S.U.
Jean Donovan
Maura Clark, M.M.
Ita Ford, M.M.

who loved the poor,
and were not afraid to share
life and death with them.

Table of Contents

Preface

Cartoon creator Tom Wilson uses some of our general impressions of Third World countries as a background for one of his famous comic strips. In that cartoon Ziggy is informed by telephone that he has won an all-expenses paid vacation to a beautiful tropical paradise. The caller hastens to reassure Ziggy that he need not have any fears about going. Despite what he might have heard, there are not half as many tarantulas as people claim; the scorpions have killed most of them. Even though the mosquitoes transmit malaria, there is nothing to worry about because they are so huge they can be seen coming a mile away. Good drinking water is not a problem either; hospital studies show the safest to be the brownish-green variety. The lucky winner is also fortunate because by the time he takes his trip, the war zone *should* have moved away from the hotel where he will be staying. The caller has just begun to mention the carnivorous lizards when Ziggy hangs up the phone and tells us that this is the first time he has ever won anything.

Having spent more than five years as a missionary in Central America, I know that the information Ziggy received concerning the living conditions in a poor tropical country was only slightly exaggerated. In our rural mission parish, I did not see many tarantulas, but each evening before I went to bed, I searched my room for any scorpions that might have wandered in that day. The mosquitoes did carry malaria, as well as a variety of other tropical diseases. After coming down with a case of typhoid fever, I learned to be very careful about the drinking water. Along with homes and highways, hotels were considered as good a place for battles, shoot outs, and bombings as any. As for the large, carnivorous lizards, well, they were there too, but I never paid much attention to them. I was more concerned about the little white lizards, whose bites were as deadly as rattlesnakes'.

The immediacy of physical danger gives a special intensity to life in a Third World country like El Salvador, where I received most of my missionary experience. In that beautiful land and under the brilliant tropical sun, people quickly realize who they are. They know almost immediately whether they are rich or poor, young or old, powerful or powerless, loving or loveless. Most clearly, they know whether their life in its most basic terms is motivated by faith, or by fear.

Before 1980, hardly any of us knew that a country named after the Saviour even existed. Now, perhaps, we might feel that we have heard enough of that country's troubles and suffering. Although it will be necessary to refer to the violence and war that has given El Salvador its recent notoriety and that continues to this day, even though it goes unreported, this book concerns another struggle, one that goes on in that country, but also within each of us. It is the struggle to live by faith, instead of by fear.

The necessity of choosing between faith and fear may not at first seem evident to us who live in a modern, complex, relatively safe, and highly technological society, where nearly everything distracts us from serious reflection, meditation, and prayer. Lost among the business of our daily activities is the awareness that what we hunger for most is a life of faith, what threatens us most is our many and varied fears.

Most of us probably will never find ourselves in exactly the same circumstances as those people whose stories are contained here. However, we should not think that the faith required of them was any greater than that which is asked of us. Our lives may differ from theirs, but our need to have faith is the same as theirs. So closely are we united with the poor in this regard that we can recognize in their stories our own struggles with faith and fear.

Until recently many of these stories could not be published because of a concern not only for the lives of the individuals, but also for the lives of their families and friends. Although many of the names of the persons in this book are fictitious, the stories told here are true stories about real persons who lived and, in some cases, died as I have recorded. These stories of these few are also the stories of many who still suffer today in Latin America.

I am deeply grateful to Sister Christine DeVinne, O.S.U., Sister Maria Berlec, O.S.U., Geraldine Kaftan, and Virginia Steigerwald for all that they did to make this book possible.

In keeping the precept of giving as gift what we have been given, all proceeds from the sale of this book will be given as a gift from you, the reader, to feed, clothe, and shelter the poor of the world.

Gifts From the Poor

> One day when Jesus was visiting the temple, He observed the people putting money into the treasury. Among the wealthy who contributed large sums was one poor widow who donated what was obviously all the money she had. Impressed by her actions, Jesus called His disciples to witness an example of true generosity and faith.[1]

Before I went to El Salvador in January of 1980 to join the Cleveland Mission Team of priests and religious and lay volunteers working there, I thought that the poor were those with material needs so great that they had nothing of value to give away. Living and working among the poor in that country, however, taught me the same lesson Jesus' disciples learned from the widow in the temple: the poor do have gifts to give.

In Central America, I saw the poor offer the little they had to those who had greater need. Frequently, the gift they gave was their last precious penny, egg, or handful of beans. I witnessed their generosity with such regularity that I knew those of us at the mission could look with confidence to the poor should we ever be in need of food.

Besides a willingness to share their food with the hungry, the poor have another, more valuable gift—faith. At times all the poor have to live on, quite literally, is their faith. Yet like the widow Jesus observed in the temple, they offer their faith as a gift to those who have eyes to see and ears to hear.

Though many centuries have come and gone, life for the poor today is comparable to what it was at the time of Jesus. In places such as our rural El Salvador parish, men and women still live and work using tools and methods that were familiar to Jesus. Women draw water from a well and carry it home in jugs balanced on their heads. Farmers clear land for planting by setting fires to burn off unwanted vegetation. They plow the earth behind a yoke of oxen and sow seeds by hand. At harvest time laborers go into the field to gather the crop. The grain they pick by hand they also separate from the chaff before storing. Fishermen pull their boats onto the beach after fishing half the night and most of the morning. They sort and sell their catch, then hang out the nets to be dried, cleaned, and repaired for the next day. Even where the implements used to make a living do not resemble those that existed in Jesus' time, the poverty that results from trying to obtain food with outdated methods does. Forced to live in areas where there is insufficient water, poor land, frequent crop failures, hazardous working environments, and high unemployment, the poor are frustrated constantly in their attempts simply to survive. Moreover, to add to their already unendurable burden of suffering, the poor are usually the first to bear the brunt of injustice and persecution.

Just as Jesus learned through his sufferings, so have the poor learned. The poor who face the same poverty as Jesus have something to tell us about faith. And when Jesus directed his disciples to observe and ponder the actions of the poor widow in the temple, he was telling us to learn from the poor as we would learn from him. Jesus grew in wisdom and grace among the poor. From his birth in a manger to his death on a cross, Jesus knew every kind of poverty. If we are not afraid to be touched by him, we can encounter Jesus today where we would have found him two thousand years ago, with the poor. To be with the poor, to observe them, to listen to them, and to learn from them is to sit at the feet of Christ and be taught by him.

What the poor have learned about faith through suffering and the grace of God, they humbly offer as a gift to us. Since as Christians we are to give what we have received as gifts to others,[2] I am compelled to pass on to you what I have learned from the poor about faith. May these stories of faith, these gifts from the poor of El Salvador, and the reflections they prompt on the life and teachings of El Salvador—"the Saviour," Jesus Christ—nourish you in your faith as they have nourished me in mine.

The Child

The living conditions I observed in rural El Salvador resembled those of the American frontier. Many of the farming families lived close to their fields and far from town. Once a week the man of the house made the journey to town in order to buy the things he did not produce. Sugar, salt, medicine, pots, tools, and matches were some of the commodities he purchased. Inevitably each farmer brought with him a young child. At first I was impressed by what seemed to be a close familial bond between father and child. When I was more familiar with the surrounding countryside, however, I doubted the wisdom of taking four and five-year-old children on such long trips. Those little ones were obviously too young to understand their father's business, and the journeys they had to endure involved hours of walking through rugged hills and tropical heat.

One day I asked a farmer why he had brought his small son on such an arduous trip. He explained that as a traveler his intentions could be misjudged. Others might misinterpret his presence or his actions as a threat. At that time in El Salvador, such a mistake often had fatal consequences. A child protected him. Even though the people he met might not be able to see his good will, they could see the child. And in the child they saw what they might doubt in him, namely, the intention to do no harm to anyone.

Children naturally possess many attractive and admirable qualities. In El Salvador, I saw the simplicity of children keep the restricted confines of a refugee camp from becoming a place of total frustration and despair. In an orphanage, I played with children who retained their innocence and ability to trust, even after they had seen the parents, brothers, and sisters brutally murdered. Despite their traumatic experiences they lived with a spiritual resilience manifested in the spark of hope in their eyes, the ring of joy in their laughter, and the warmth of love in their embraces. Children everywhere share a playful spirit that defies description. They all speak the universal language of smiles, winks, and hugs. They all understand the games of tease, tickle, and catch-me-if-you-can. Admittedly, youngsters can at times be anything but angelic. However, they have an engaging freshness that redeems even their temperamental and tearful moments. Aside from all these characteristics, one quality uniquely belongs to them—the ability to be nonthreatening.

The common folk of El Salvador value more than any other quality in children this nonthreatening nature. On numerous occasions they have seen the mere presence of a child forestall hostility and violence. Children evoke from the belligerent and malicious something of their better selves. Sometimes it is restraint; sometimes, compassion; sometimes, mercy. Children have this effect on others because they naturally communicate a defenselessness, an inability to harm, and a dependence upon the good will of others. They do this so well that they often save their own lives and the lives of those who are in their company.

When Jesus called a child to stand in the midst of a group of adults, it was to show them a person who is nonthreatening.[1] Children, simply by being who they are, free us to be gentler, more understanding, and more compassionate with them than we usually are with adults. Knowing how we are with children, Jesus points to a child as an example of what we have to become. If we are to enter the Kingdom of God, we must become like children, who, by not threatening those around them, call forth the best from others.

We better appreciate what Jesus invites us *to*, if we understand what he invites us *from*. Through the course of even one day, we each receive any number of emotional beatings. The psychological thumps, bumps, and lumps we sustain in our ordinary dealings with others can take their toll on us. When these unpleasant encounters with others magnify deeper and more personal hurts, we tend to view life as fundamentally painful. Not wanting to be hurt anymore, we construct various kinds of protective barriers around ourselves. Like the strategies and weapons of superpowers in an arms race, our defense mechanisms gradually become more numerous and more sophisticated. Before too long, we become quite good at protecting ourselves emotionally. We develop our personal defense systems to a degree that allows us effectively and selectively to shut out anyone we choose, even God, for as long as we like. We fail to realize in all of this, however, that we are the victims of our own strategies. The defenses we erect to protect ourselves threaten those who see them. Frightened by these defenses, they rush off to build their own. Their defenses, in turn, only scare us into more self-isolation and self-protection.

Allowing ourselves to be caught in this escalating cycle of defense and counterdefense, we plod through life under the illusion that we can save ourselves by our own devices. Instead of freeing ourselves from needless pain and hurt, we make ourselves the prisoners of our own fears and insecurities. Instead of opening ourselves to the beauty of creation, we lock ourselves in dungeons of worry and anxiety. Most tragic of all, instead of letting the light of our goodness shine for all to see, we cover it with layer upon layer of defenses. We bury our goodness so deeply within ourselves that even we lose sight of it. Defensiveness, imprisonment, fear—Jesus invites us away from these.

What Christ invites us *to,* he shows us by coming here first as a child and then as bread. Few if any things in this world are less threatening than a small child and a piece of bread. By approaching us as a child and as bread, God's intent is that we not be frightened away. That God is nonthreatening and loves us is good news. Indeed, it is the best news ever. In order that this good news might effectively be preached to all the nations, Jesus insists that his disciples be nonthreatening, like him. When we go on a missionary journey, we are to travel without gold, silver, haversack, spare tunic, footwear, or staff.[2] In other words, we are to take nothing that would in any way influence, impress, or intimidate others, nothing that might pressure our listeners into accepting the message we preach. The Good News is to be proclaimed freely and to be received freely, and the disciples that do this best offer no threat to anyone. In proclaiming the Good News, we are to be like children, who are defenseless, who are dependent upon the good will of others, and who desire only peace for those they meet.

Contrary to popular belief, being defenseless does not make us vulnerable. We are vulnerable only when we have something to defend. Being defenseless—that is, having nothing that we must defend—is pure strength. Considering all as loss, we have nothing that others can use or strike at to hurt us. Being defenseless does not mean, however, that we have nothing at all upon which to base our lives. In becoming nonthreatening we ground our lives in what cannot be destroyed or taken away from us. That indestructible source of our lives is God's love for us. Since nothing can separate us from the love of Christ,[3] we need not defend it out of fear that we will lose it. We cannot lose God's love. We always have it. We must always depend on it to free us from being vulnerable.

Having spent years building our defenses, we need time to dismantle them. We also need time to become like children. Neither of these tasks is easy. While acquiring the child's ability to be nonthreatening, we will still have feelings that others will trample. Some people will misjudge our actions and attribute an evil design to them. Some people will take advantage of our kindness. Still others will treat us disgracefully, as though our unselfish deeds cause them pain instead of comfort.

Of those people who will deal with us shamefully some will want us out of their sight. They will drive us away as, in the Gospels, the Gerasenes drive Jesus from their land.[4] In that account Jesus transforms a demoniac who terrorized the countryside into a gentle man. Supposedly, the Gerasenes no longer have anything to fear from the ex-demoniac. But they still are afraid of him. The change in him frightens them. Instead of being afraid of him because he threatens them with violence, they are now afraid of him because he does not threaten them at all. Scared that Jesus might ask them to live in the same gentle and nonthreatening way, they beg him to leave them alone. Upon their insistence, Jesus departs, but not without sending someone to live among the Gerasenes as a reminder of what God has done that day. Jesus tells the man from who he had exorcised the evil spirits to stay in that region. His discipleship is to give witness to the invitation Jesus had delivered to the people, the invitation to become like children and belong to the Kingdom.

Lastly, there are those people who will do much worse to us than simply send us away. Although the nonthreatening qualities of a child encourage many people to reveal what is most beautifully human and divine in them, for those with malicious hearts that innocence is the greatest of all threats. From King Herod's murder of children in the time of Jesus[5] to the slaughter of uncounted thousands in our century, history teaches us a chilling fact: there are those who will not turn from their evil goals even for the sake of the innocent and the childlike.

The diabolical reaction of some people to our efforts to be Christ-like might discourage us, if it were not for the unexpected love of God. In being nonthreatening, God is the master of the unexpected. No one expected God to come as a child, or to save us in the way that he did, or to be our Bread of Life. In mastering the fine art of being like a child, we too are to do the unexpected. When others expect us to be hostile towards them, we stand unarmed before them. When others do not expect us to be kind to them, we show them love.[6] When others do not expect forgiveness, we are generous with pardon and mercy.[7] When others do not see anything in which to hope, we have hope.[8]

Just as Jesus placed a child in the middle of a group of adults, he places us in the midst of this world. To most people, responding like defenseless and unprotected children is considered foolish; to Christ, it is belonging to the Kingdom.[9] Surrounded by harshness and violence, we are to expect others to be good. Our faith in their goodness will not always keep us from harm. But by being nonthreatening like children, we will call forth the best from others and be the world's only real hope for unity.

The Lost

Some of the saddest words heard in Central and South America today are *los desaparecidos*. This Spanish phrase literally means "those who have disappeared." The people of Latin America use this term when referring to the men, women, and children who were taken from their families by force and have never returned. Uncounted thousands have disappeared. In our part of Central America, every one of us knew people who vanished, often without a trace. One day they were living and working among us, and the next they were missing. Sometimes we found their tortured bodies along the roadside or in shallow graves. Most of the time, we were left only with the emptiness of their absence. We mourned losing them. We puzzled over who had taken them and why. The only thing we knew was that once someone disappeared, it was extremely unlikely that we would ever see or hear from that person again. To be missing was to be lost.

While I was in Central America I spoke with one man, a rare individual, who had been abducted but lived to tell about it. I wanted to hear his story not only because it was unique, but also because I had a vested interest in knowing his thoughts. A few months prior to his kidnapping, we had found the bodies of four friends in an unmarked grave. Having wondered what their last thoughts might have been, I hoped that the man's description of his experience would give me some insight into what might have crossed my friends' minds before they were killed.

The man told me how a group of armed men

surprised him, bound him hand and foot, threw him into the back of a truck, and drove away with him. His most vivid recollection was the fear that his disappearance had been unnoticed. He also remembered hoping that someone had witnessed his capture and was at that moment telling his family. The longer he was a captive, though, the dimmer was his hope of seeing his wife and children again.

One day during that man's ordeal, severe depression overcame him. Strangely enough, while he stood on the brink of despair, he felt as though his death was no longer in the hands of his tormentors. The choice of whether he lived or died was his to make. He could choose to believe that someone was going to rescue him, and live. Or he could choose to give up all hope of being saved, and die. He was not sure exactly who was going to save him. But he knew that if he was to live, he would have to believe in someone.

As it turned out, several people rescued the man. Although he was overjoyed to be free, the man admitted that seeing the faces of his rescuers was not as important for him as believing during his captivity that someone was searching for him. That hope kept him alive through the days and nights of pain and torture. "I knew," the man testified, "that the moment I stopped having faith that someone was coming for me, I would die right then and there. And there would have been no one left to rescue."

Those of us who were present for the return of this *desaparecido* to his family will never forget what we experienced. So rarely did that event occur in El Salvador that to see a person who had disappeared come back to the embrace of his family was to see

> someone who had risen from the grave. Joy filled us completely. Joy for him. Joy for his family. We thought of nothing else at that moment but rejoicing with his family and friends over the miraculous homecoming of a man who had been lost.

In a trio of parables Jesus three times describes the joy of God's Kingdom as the joy of finding what is lost.[1] In those parables "lost" means more than temporarily or absent-mindedly misplaced; "found," more than discovered by chance. To be lost is to be dead; to be found is to be brought back to life. Therefore whether it is a sheep, a coin, or a son, finding what is lost is an occasion that calls for rejoicing. "Let us eat and celebrate," exclaims the father upon the return of the prodigal, "because this son of mine was dead and has come back to life. He was lost and is found."[2]

God gives the joy of the Kingdom to all who belong to it. Yes sometimes we experience little or no joy in life and wonder why there is not more joy in the world. While we understand the simply stated commandments of God, the exhortation to "rejoice always"[3] befuddles us.

Sometimes the reason for our joylessness is that we have chosen the wrong role in our relationship to God. God is the one who has come to search out and save what is lost; we are the ones God seeks.[4] Our joy is in being found. God's joy and the joy of all the Kingdom is in finding us. When we forget this and attempt to reverse roles with God, we distort our relationship with God. Confusing who God is with who we are always causes unnecessary anxiety and sorrow. We are like a little boy who wandered away from his mother. When he realized that she was not standing behind him, he believed that she was the one who was lost. Foolishly and frantically he ran in every direction trying to find her. All the while the boy was unaware that it was he who was lost and the object of an earnest search.

In our relationship with the divine, God is not the one who gets lost. We are. We are the lost sheep, the lost coin, and the lost son of Jesus' parables. God is the finder. Unfortunately, like the little boy who searched for his "lost" mother, we usually prefer to see ourselves in the active role of finder rather than the passive one of being found. We have difficulty seeing ourselves as the ones who are lost. When we talk about our relationship with God, we often express our need for God as the need to find God. Approaching God as if God were the one who was lost is not, however, the way to the joy of the Kingdom.

Fortunately God finds us, even in spite of ourselves. Rather than belittle or degrade us for getting lost, God lavishes upon us divine concern, love, and affection. That is God's way. God makes us the focal point of love. If we are to realize the love God has for us, we must believe that God will find us whenever we are lost.

Some of the wisest words on the subject of lost-and-found were spoken by a father to his four children. He instructed them on what to do if they ever became lost. He told them about seeking help and whom they could trust. He warned them about keeping away from danger and never going into strange places by themselves. Punctuating his remarks, though, were these words of guidance and promise: "In the event that you are lost, stay where you are and I will come and find you." By obeying their father, the children would facilitate his search for them and thus help to diminish the time that they were apart from him. By believing their father's words, the children would remain calm and be able to control their fear because they knew that their father loved them and would come for them.

We are lost when we believe other than what Jesus has told us. One of the many untruths we frequently believe is that we are alone. Another untruth is that we are unloved. A third is that we are unlovable. None of these beliefs is true, but many of us believe that they all are, solely on the strength of our feelings. In these cases we are not to believe our feelings as if they were the source of truth. Feelings are to be felt. The Word of God is to be believed.

Through his Word, God informs us that there is more to creation than what we perceive through our senses and emotions. Despite what we may feel, we are not prisoners in a runaway universe. We are not alone and unloved in the world. We are much loved by God and by others. If we do feel his care and tenderness, we are to consider that a blessing and enjoy it. If we do not have the sensation that God is near, we ought not believe that God loves us any less. God's love for us does not depend on how we feel. In other words, our feelings do not measure or control; nor do they limit or define God's love. We need not try to escape, deny, or suppress feelings that we do not like or that contradict God's Word. We let them be. We stay where we are, so to speak. In the midst of every feeling or emotion, we calmly and confidently believe what Jesus has communicated to us about God's never ending love. To believe the Good News that we are not alone, that we are loved and lovable, is not easy, especially when we feel otherwise. As with all things worth doing, however, we should not use the difficulty of believing as an excuse for refusing to put our faith in God.

We see the difference that placing faith before feeling makes in our lives by looking at the way Jesus approached prayer. When Jesus prayed, he went to a lonely place—a desert, a mountain, the wilderness. Generally, we find such places too solitary for our own tastes. If we rely solely on our feelings to move us toward those secluded spots, we seldom arrive there. Even if we do choose to go to a lonely place in order to pray, we do not go very often or for very long. Those kinds of places frighten us. We get lost in them. In them we suffer both physically and emotionally. Like the people of Jesus' time, we are reluctant to leave the busy market in order to chance a meeting with God in an out of the way place. We prefer to be where everyone else is and have our encounters with God among them. Following God into a lonely place is not our idea of where God or we should be.[5] Whereas our feelings lead us to believe that we are alone in those deserted locations, Jesus believed he was never alone.[6] Jesus did not go away from everyone to be by himself. He went to be with his Father. Jesus believed that his Father was always with him. That belief was so vital for his life on earth that when he left, he gave his followers the same assurance of his continuing presence. As he ascended to the right hand of his Father, Jesus promised to be with us until the end of time.[7]

God intentionally calls us into solitude in order to fashion for us a new heart and to teach us the extent of love. If no desert or mountain or wilderness is at hand, God will meet us in a room behind a closed door.[8] We know from experience, though, that deserts and empty rooms are not the only desolate spots in our lives. Lonely places and times have a way of finding us. They creep up on us and surprise us when we least expect them. In a crowd, at a party, at home, and in that part of our heart that no one has yet touched, we can suddenly be more alone and lost than if we were stranded on a forgotten island in the middle of a boundless sea. Jesus invites us not to run away from any of those lonely moments, but to live through them with faith. We never need to fear these experiences, because no matter how unlikely it seems, we can meet God in all of them. Jesus knows every place and every feeling in which we can get lost. He has prayed in every one of them, and he knows where to find us. Christ transforms lonely places and moments of isolation into a rendezvous between the divine and the human. In those places, we shall know the joy of the Kingdom if we, the lost, believe in Christ, the finder.

The joy of the Kingdom, wherever it overtakes us, is purely a gift.[9] Acknowledging our lostness and trusting that God will find us prepares us for receiving that gift. When we receive it, our joy indicates that God always knows exactly where we are and is already at our side. Even when we face death, as did my four friends and all those who have disappeared in Latin America, we will not be lost as long as we have faith in that divine finder who is God. To be sure, our feelings will often resist the truth our faith brings us. More and more, however, we shall win our feelings over to the truth as we continue to put our trust in the Word of God. His word to us is that we are not lost. We are not alone. God is with us! We are loved! We are found! Let us rejoice!

The Widow

The old woman who walked slowly across the town plaza early one morning in the middle of the dry season was a widow. She was one of the many Latin American widows who personify poverty. Her home was a one room hut made of sticks, with a grass roof and a dirt floor. No one lived with her or provided for her. She managed to eke out an existence by selling a few vegetables each day. She had no idea what she was going to do when age and infirmity confined her to a bed. Although she worried about that day, she went into the office of the town's commandant with a more immediate concern.

The widow's visit was no surprise to the military officer. Several times a day for the past two days he had faced the widow and her unchanging plea. She begged for the release of a certain young man whom he was detaining. A team of recruiters had drafted the youth on a recent sweep through the town. Since the youth did not qualify for a deferment, the commandant was holding him until he could arrange to have him transported to the army's training camp. The youth was not a relative of the widow, but he had befriended her and had been an asset to the community in general. Not wanting to see him taken from the village, the widow decided to do everything in her power to get him released from his military duty. The poor, however, have only one course of action available to them—persistent petition. A lifetime of poverty had perfected the widow's skill at petitioning and had made her more persistent than most. For the past two full days, the widow had done nothing but ask

> to talk to the commandant. Every time she stood before the officer, she repeated her request until, his patience worn out, he ordered the guards to escort her out of the building. Undaunted, the determined widow returned again and again to secure the young man's freedom.
>
> At noon on the third day, the widow emerged from the commandant's headquarters. This time, however, she was not flanked by a pair of guards. She was in the company of the liberated young man. The widow, with her persistent petitioning, accomplished what the townspeople thought could not be done.

In the widow who won the young man's freedom, the townspeople saw another woman. She was the widow in the Gospel of Luke, who sought justice from an unscrupulous judge.[1] Confronted with a similar situation, the widow of our village took the same course of action as the woman in Jesus' parable. Petitioning as persistent as hers Jesus called prayer.

The poor must petition in order to survive. Without wealth or influence, without anyone to speak for them or champion their cause, the poor must contend with poverty as though it were a personal adversary. Poverty is unrelenting in its pursuit of the poor. Ruthless, it stalks the poor and seeks their destruction. It frustrates their attempts to survive and blocks their chances to prosper. Poverty subjects the poor to untold suffering and the constant threat of death. It denies the poor even a moment's peace as it drives them into an early grave. The poor have no defense to combat poverty except to petition for what they need. Since their existence depends upon petition, asking, knocking, and seeking are a way of life for them.

The poor sustain their petitioning with faith. They believe that their pleas will be answered. Because poverty will not go away, the poor can never cease their asking. They must persist. If they lose heart and quit petitioning, they soon lose their lives.

Besides trusting the power of petition, the poor also put their faith in the person from whom they seek help. Since they fully expect that person to give them what they need, they are persistent in the way they ask. The poor are like the man in Luke's gospel who knocks on his neighbor's door late one night.[2] An unexpected guest has arrived at his house. Not being able to meet the needs of the traveler, the man has sought aid from his neighbor. If the man seems to be inconsiderate towards his neighbor in the way he asks for bread, that is how the poor are. Their need is urgent. They have no time for amenities. Poverty does not allow them to observe social courtesies. Even if it seems that the benefactor whose rest they disturb may deny their request, the poor must keep asking until the need is met.

As the poor need to petition, we need to pray. It is true that life depends upon prayerful petition, not only for those who suffer great material want, but also for every one of us. Before God, we are all poor. We are more dependent upon God for life than the poor are dependent upon charity for survival. Believing that life could easily go on without prayer is a mistake. To have life in its completeness, we cannot treat prayer as though it were a kind of religious hobby or a Sunday affair. We cannot say to ourselves that we will turn to prayer once we have finished the more important business of everyday life or when we need something and cannot get it in any other way. Prayer is indispensable for life. If we do not pray well, we do not live well. Life slips away from us if our prayer is not urgent, intense, and constant. Only by praying persistently will life be for us ever new, fresh, and crisp.

When Jesus' own life was at stake, he chose to pray in the manner of the poor. In the Garden of Gethsemane, Jesus, utterly poor and alone, petitioned his Father to deliver him from suffering death. Like the poor, Jesus petitioned his Father more than once. He returned to pray a second time. And a third. Each time he prayed, he used the same petition, the same few words, over and over. "Abba (O Father), you have the power to do all things. Take this cup away from me. But let it be as you would have it, not as I."[3] Even though the cup of suffering remained, Jesus did not lose heart. He kept praying. In the garden and on the cross. And the Father answered Jesus' persistent prayer of faith with life and resurrection.

In order to share in the life Christ received from his Father, we too must be faithful, pray always, and never lose heart. Once we learn to pray as Christ did, prayer will be more than just one of many courses of action we might take when we have a problem to solve or a situation to correct. It will be more than the last resort when all else has failed. In all things, our recourse will be to prayer. If there is need for petitions to God, prayer would have us propose them with trust and confidence. If there is need for action to be taken, prayer will inspire and sustain us in what we must do.

We pray best when, like the poor, we take seriously Jesus' words, "Ask and you shall receive."[4] Without the fear of being disappointed, we are to ask boldly and repeatedly for what is needed. Like the widow before the unscrupulous judge, the man outside his neighbor's door, and the widow in the office of the commandant, we are never to stop asking.

With God, how we ask is more important than what we ask. In other words, our praying is more important than our specific requests. God is the Father we can trust. Like a good father, he knows better than we do what we need and what is good for us. Like a loving mother, she wants to give to her children all that will benefit us. In order that we might receive from her, she says that we have only to ask. If we pray with faithfulness and persistence, we shall receive. Because we can rely upon God, we are assured that what we shall receive from God will always come out of love for us and will always give us life.

The Vigilant

Living in El Salvador demanded vigilance. We constantly had to be on the look out for potentially dangerous situations. Clashes between government troops and guerrillas could erupt anywhere and at any time. San Salvador, the capital, offered its own brand of danger. There, as in the other major cities, bombs exploded randomly and without warning, killing people, gutting buildings, and leaving a carpet of broken glass in the street. We never went to the capital without wondering if we were going to be in the wrong place at the wrong time. Driving across the countryside was like making a trip through a battlefield. Being caught in a deadly crossfire was always a possibility and one of our greatest fears. The rural town in which we lived changed hands numerous times during El Salvador's civil war. Although many of the takeovers were peaceful, extensive gunfire and grenade explosions preceded several of them. In addition to this, we frequently awoke at night to the sound of shooting. In the morning we would hear the sad stories of what had happened, who had been killed, who was missing.

All was not war, though. There were periods so quiet and calm that we almost forgot about the violence in that beautiful land. Those times, however, did not last long enough. Just as we began to think that the situation was improving, the detonation of a bomb or a burst of rifle fire put us back on the alert for imminent danger.

The threat of violence and death took its toll on us. Fear hit us in waves and eroded our sense of security. When the level of fear in the community was high, our caution bordered on panic. We deserted the streets a few minutes earlier each evening. Hoping that the violence would pass us by, we shut our doors, locked our windows and huddled in our homes. When our anxiety did subside, we emerged from our hiding places and tried to live a normal existence. We attempted to forget our fear and deny the danger we were in by telling ourselves and others that it was nothing. If it were not for a gentleman named José, we might have gone on believing that we were brave, when in fact we were acting quite foolishly.

José was a poor peasant, and like many of his fellow dirt farmers, he was generous to a fault. What distinguished him from the rest was the peace and control he maintained over himself even in the most frightening times. José was not blind to the dangers. He was very much aware of what could have happened to us all. Yet in spite of everything, he emanated a peace we all envied. When our nerves could no longer take the tension caused by the proximity of peril, we looked to him for reassurance. His presence had a calming effect on us. If asked what kept him from falling apart under the stress of the difficult living conditions, José could give it no other name than faith.

José taught us much about vigilance. He showed us that there are different kinds. One type of vigilance is occasional in nature. The immediate threat of danger motivates it. When danger is near, the level of this vigilance is high. When there is no danger, there is little or no vigilance. Because this kind of vigilance has an on-again, off-again character, the occasionally vigilant ride an emotional roller coaster. As tension rises, so does their anxiety. The longer the tension lasts, the more their nerves are strained until either they or the situation breaks. As the cause for their fear diminishes and life returns to what it was, they breathe a sigh of relief and slowly regain their composure. When the reason for alarm has passed, they either forget or deny that they were in real danger until the next time their lives are threatened.

By nature the occasionally vigilant only watch for a particular event. If what they are waiting for is something they want to happen, they are anxious about missing it. If the event is some evil or disaster, they are convinced they will not escape it. While it may be better to be one of the occasionally vigilant than one of the "worthless" lot who do not keep any vigil,[1] it is still not an enviable way to live. The occasionally vigilant eventually develop the habits of looking over their shoulders for destruction, seeing death in every shadow, and expecting disaster to hit at any moment. A dreadful sense of impending doom spoils what enjoyment they find in life. Or even worse, if what they are waiting for does not occur right away, they cease their vigilance. With their guard down, the occasionally vigilant are frequently surprised by the very thing they no longer expect to happen.

In a parable about vigilance, Jesus likens those who are occasionally vigilant to five foolish virgins who await the arrival of a bridegroom. They begin to watch for him but soon fall asleep. When the moment they are waiting for approaches, it catches them by surprise. They awaken to the realization that they do not have the resources for a long and sustained vigil. Because they did not prepare to keep the right kind of vigilance, they miss the bridegrooms' appearance and the celebration that follows.[2]

In contrast to vigilance that is occasional and intermittent, José demonstrated for us another kind, which is constant in nature. The scriptures describe the constantly vigilant as "awake," "alert," "watching," and "on guard." Just as the five wise virgins in Jesus' parable did not differ in their outward appearance from the five foolish virgins, so the constantly vigilant do not differ outwardly from the occasionally vigilant. They take the same precautions in time of peril that others do. They leave the streets when everyone else does. They bolt their doors and lock their windows like everyone else. They differ from the rest, however, in that they carry out all the necessary safety measure without a sense of panic. They are not frantic. They act with quiet assurance. In spite of the threat of danger, they exhibit an unshakable peace. The constantly vigilant are peaceful because avoiding personal harm is not their only concern. They are alert and ready to respond with faith to whatever life may bring, be it blessing or trial. The constantly vigilant are always wakeful. They are not caught off guard by life's unpredictable twists and tragic times. Even while they sleep, they are always awake to the possibility that greater faith may be asked of them at anytime. As did the five wise virgins, they keep their lamps burning brightly in anticipation of seeing an opportunity to act with faith in the next set of circumstances that comes along.

With good reason Jesus Christ tells us to watch and pray.[3] Prayer is the oil in the lamp of vigilance. Prayer enables us to see. Prayer is revelatory. It alerts us to the presence of God and opens our eyes to God's identity. It awakens us to who we are and enlightens us to the true nature of the times in which we live. In the Scriptures, for instance, Jesus' identity is frequently revealed in the context of prayer. The two persons who first identify Jesus as the Anointed One are the deeply prayerful Simeon and Anna.[4] It is while Jesus is praying after his baptism by John that the Holy Spirit publicly reveals that the Son of God is among the people.[5] In the context of private prayer, Jesus questions his apostles about his identity, and Peter shows that he knows that he is the Messiah.[6] And it is while Jesus and three of his disciples are praying on a mountain that the Son of God reveals himself to them in the Transfiguration.[7]

A prayerful vigilance is easier to maintain in some countries than in others. Those who reside in places like El Salvador have cause to be more vigilant. They know from personal experience that anything can happen. Those of us who live in First World countries, however, like the United States, are in much greater danger than those who live in Third World nations torn by revolution. Our lives are in peril because of our tendency to think that we are safe and have little need to keep watch. Like the rich man in the Gospel of Luke, we become brainwashed by security.[8] We believe that we can assure our own happiness by careful planning and that we can store up wealth for our own enjoyment. Oh, we nod our heads and admit that theoretically we might die at anytime, yet we go on programming ourselves to think and act as if we will live to a ripe old age. Nothing manifests this better than our own reactions to the death of a young person we have known and loved. We feel as if we have been cheated of that person's presence in our lives. In truth we may very well have suffered an injustice, but the injustice would not have come from the hand of God. In the midst of our grief or anger, we must ask ourselves: Who guaranteed that anyone of us should live for a specified amount of time? Who decreed that we would live a full life before we died? If we think that God has given us an agreement about how long we will live, we are as foolish as the rich man, who, on the night he thought his life was secure, had to depart this world.

God does not guarantee anything to us in the way of time, because time is not the measure of happiness. God does promise to us, however, something more valuable than time. God promises that we will have God's faithfulness and love every minute of our lives. It is the security we have in this promise of God, and not in the number of years we live on earth, that gives peace to our soul. Ultimately, God's faithfulness and love are what the vigilant watch for and the reason why they pray. God's faithful love is like a priceless pearl.[9] The vigilant watch for its appearance and are willing to sacrifice everything in faith in order to have it. Such a love is worth treasuring, for it not only brings peace but also gives meaning and value to life no matter how long or short that life might be. If we pass the time we have in this world depending on God's faithfulness and love, we shall not have lived in vain.

Let us make no mistake. There are other promises around besides God's. The world promises peace and security, too—through the accumulation of riches and arms. There always seems to be a need for one more weapon to be developed, a little more money to be acquired, or one more war to be fought before we will have the peace promised by the powers of the world. We ought to know by now that peace and security cannot be acquired by possessing wealth and weapons. It was evident to us in El Salvador that peace resides within those vigilant people, like our friend José, who watch and pray. Those of us who are ready to respond with faith in any situation and who keep a constant vigil for God's love and faithfulness will do better than know peace. We will be the ones who bring peace to the world.

The Fisherman

> The fisherman was poorly clad. Shoeless and shirtless, he stood on the beach in a pair of frayed pants held up by a cord belt. His only adornment hung from a piece of fishing line around his neck. It was a small metal crucifix that was as worn and weatherbeaten as he was. The fisherman took pride in showing me his boat. It was a single piece of wood, a carefully selected tree trunk, cut and shaped to make a seaworthy vessel. As he ran his hand along the gunwale, he told me that he had once been caught in a sudden storm. Only faith in himself and in his boat had brought him back home alive.
>
> The fisherman had lived by the sea all his life, and out of curiosity I asked him if he had ever learned to swim. His reply suggested that his thoughts were still on that storm he had survived. Solemnly and unabashedly he held up the metal crucifix and said, "When a storm becomes more than me and my boat can handle, I put myself in God's hands."

Although a carpenter by trade, Jesus had a seaman's love for boats. He frequently traveled in them. He preached from them and taught in them. He felt so at home in them that he could sleep soundly even when his boat was in heavy seas. Transportation, pulpit, classroom, resting place—for Jesus a boat was many things. But most of all, a boat at sea was a place where faith and fear met. In a pair of sea adventures, the storm on the lake[1] and Peter's walk on the water,[2] Jesus used his disciples' familiarity with boats to expose their faith and their fears. At sea Jesus showed the disciples that while faith in themselves and their boats served them well enough in making a living, they needed to act with greater faith and less fear if they wanted to be his disciples.

Most of the disciples were seasoned sailors. They relied routinely on their abilities and their boats to get them through any weather. During the storm on the lake, however, all their strength and skills could not save them. On that occasion they were no match for the elements. They were badly beaten by nature's force, and they knew it. By the time the disciples woke the sleeping Jesus, the wind had blown away their confidence, and the waves that broke over them had washed away their hope of survival. In the eyes of those soaked and forlorn men, Jesus saw only defeat and despair. According to some accounts, the disciples had simply given up. What faith they had in themselves and in their boat was crushed. When they realized that their boat was going down and they could not stop it from sinking, the disciples concluded that their lives were lost with it. So certain were they of their end that they did not even bother to ask Jesus to save them. They had awakened him only to tell him the bad news. Jesus reprimanded them for the way they were behaving. The bad news was not that they were perishing. The bad news was that they were men of little faith.

Through a second sea adventure, Jesus again exhorted his disciples to have less faith in their boats and more faith in him. In that dramatic scene, Jesus was walking on the water and he invited Peter to join him. At that time, the faith of Peter and the other disciples was young and still immature. Their faith was like the seed that had fallen on rocky ground;[3] it could just as quickly die. With an exuberant display of faith, Peter jumped from his boat and started walking on the water towards Jesus. Peter, however, soon regretted what he had done.

Peter had never seen the sea from any vantage point other than the security of the shore or the deck of a ship. Nothing in his life had prepared him to be standing where he was at that moment. He was the first and only person in history to walk away from a boat while it was still at sea. Observing the strength of the wind and the waves, Peter grew increasingly uneasy. With nothing solid under his feet, Peter began to have second thoughts about what he was doing. He was a fisherman and a seaman. Being in a boat was second nature to him. Everything that a lifetime of sailing had engrained in him was in conflict with his new faith in Jesus. All of a sudden he wanted to go back to his boat, to the world he knew and understood, the world in which he felt secure. But Peter had just enough faith that he also feared turning his back on Jesus and making a desperate lunge for his boat. Peter was torn between his boat and his Lord. Part of him wanted to look to his boat for salvation. Part of him said, "Forget about your boat and trust yourself to Christ." Choking on sea water and indecision, Peter nearly drowned. He would have drowned if not for a certain memory and a decision. Having been close to a watery grave on a previous occasion, Peter remembered that incident and what he had learned from it. Before it was too late, Peter did what he and his fellow disciples did not do when their boat was sinking beneath the waves. He called out to Jesus. With a cry of "Lord, save me!"[4] he abandoned the boat he had been taught from birth to trust and entrusted himself to Christ's care. Peter was not disappointed in his choice. Just as Jesus had done in the midst of the storm on the lake, he put out his hand and restored life.

Although we may not be fishermen or sailors, we all have boats. Our boats are those people, places, pastimes, professions, projects, and prizes from which we derive our security, self-worth, and sense of wholeness. More often than not, these boats of ours are gifts from God. Therefore, it is more appropriate to call them "lifeboats," for they enable us to enjoy the good times in life more completely and to weather the hard times in life more assuredly. If it were not for such life-giving boats, we would not fare well in this world.

It is the law of the sea and of God, however, that on certain occasions, we must abandon ship in order to live. As good as our boats might be, none of them can be a substitute for God. Our boats are not all-powerful or unsinkable. Nor will they last forever. To expect more of them than they are capable of giving is a fatal mistake. When one of our boats comes between God and us, faith requires that we either alter our relationship with that particular boat so we no longer rely on it more than God, or that we abandon it altogether.

Just as there are times when we must abandon a boat, there are also times when a boat abandons us. We may see the loss of a boat coming and even be able to predict it. On the other hand, the loss of someone or something dear to us may happen mysteriously, suddenly, and apparently for no reason. No matter what the circumstances are that surround the loss of one or more of our boats, the experience is generally the same. Like the disciples in their floundering boat, we realize that we are powerless to stop or change what is happening. We feel the chilling touch of fear. We panic when we see that which we depended upon, loved, and called our life slip away from us. Because we identify much of our existence with that boat, we conclude that we are lost if it is.

During times of loss, when we need God the most, God can seem to be unaware of our pain. It can seem as if God is asleep as Jesus was in the disciples' sinking boat. Perhaps Jesus is asleep, or at least has his eyes closed, because he does not want to watch us destroy ourselves by hanging on stubbornly to what is already lost. In any event, when we cannot prevent the loss from occurring, faith is often a matter of letting go and trusting God to fill the voids and vacancies in our lives. Like the disciples we must learn and remember that salvation and peace are found not in any boat but in the God whom the winds and the waves obey.

From the time Jesus first called the disciples,[5] the summons to follow him has always meant leaving behind certain good boats. If we answer his call, Jesus gently helps us to perfect our faith. He affirms us with the same intensity of feeling for him that prompted the first disciples to leave their boats on the shore and Peter to abandon his at sea in order to be with him. He blesses us with moments of excitement, exhilaration, joy, and peace over having left all for him. And as Jesus saved the disciples' boat from sinking and restored Peter to his, our Lord may return to us a boat we have lost or give us a boat we never expected to have, just to assure us of his presence and his love for us.

While Jesus would have us be certain of his constant presence in our lives, to grow in faith will often be a painful experience for us. Like Peter when he was lost in the sea, we too will wonder if we have made a mistake by leaving everything to follow Christ. In times of doubt and indecision it will appear to us that our salvation rests in assurances that are more concrete, more human, than those which Jesus offers. We will be greatly tempted to alter, change, or forget our commitment to Christ in order to seek our own security, our own safe harbor. Considering what we suffer when Christ calls us to abandonment, it is not surprising that many people are reluctant to answer our Lord when he beckons them. The general public looks upon a life-long, faith-filled discipleship in much the same way that it looks at walking on water: it would be wonderful if it could be done, but practically speaking it is impossible. With God, however, all things are possible. In the midst of any storm of conflicting thoughts and emotions, we must not repeat Peter's mistake of taking our eyes off our Lord. The only real danger we face in life is in looking for a way to save ourselves instead of renewing our faith in God.

Through repeated acts of abandonment, Peter perfected his response to Christ's call. During his earthly association with Jesus, Peter had plenty of practice at abandoning his boat. At the start of Jesus' ministry, the Lord called Peter to leave his boat on the shore and follow him. While at sea, Jesus beckoned Peter to forsake his boat and come to him across the water. After the Resurrection, Jesus, by his presence on the shore of the Sea of Galilee, called Peter once more from his boat.[6] With the exuberance that was reminiscent of earlier responses, the disciple leapt from his boat. But that time he did not falter on his way to Christ, as he had previously. He lunged through the water that separated him from the Risen Lord without any doubt that he would find in him all he needed for life. In this last abandonment of his boat, Peter accomplished what he had promised to do in the first. He left his boat, never to return to it, in order to have life in Christ.

In a similar manner, Jesus continually calls us to leave everything and follow him. He will purify and perfect our initial responses to him through repeated calls to discipleship. The acts of radical abandonment that a life of faith requires may seem foolish to some and impossible to others. But to those who have heard Christ's call and have experienced life with him, there simply is no other way to live.

Because my fisherman friend had told me about his faith, I believed that he was at peace when we committed his body, with its weathered metal crucifix, to the earth. He did run into a storm that he and his boat could not survive. The storm, however, was not one of nature, but rather one of the man-made variety we call "war." He had been fishing in a river not far from where it emptied into the sea, when he pulled up a lost grenade in his net. As he tried to free it, the bomb exploded and killed him and a companion.

When news of the fisherman's death first reached me, I thought of the time we met on the beach and what he had said to me. Now, whenever life becomes tempestuous for me, I repeat his words to myself:

> "When a storm becomes more than me and my
> boat can handle, I put myself in God's hands."

The Unafraid

At one time or another, the war in El Salvador touched every part of our mission parish. But the area hardest hit was the hill country to the west of town. The battles between government troops and the rebels in that region put the inhabitants under a terrible strain. One farmer in particular showed the effects of constantly living in fear for one's life. When he talked to us, his eyes nervously darted about in a constant lookout for danger. His hands trembled uncontrollably, and he spoke in guarded whispers. Like many other farmers, he did not want war. He wanted to be left in peace to work the land and to provide for his family. The farmer was scared because he was under a great deal of pressure both from the soldiers and from the guerrillas. Each group wanted him to join it to rid the country of the other. The farmer tried to remain neutral but the day was fast approaching when he would be forced to declare his allegiance. He worried that if he publicly professed which side he supported, the other side might see to it that he regretted his choice. For the farmer, there seemed to be no escape. Even his poverty did not give him any alternatives. He could leave his fields and become a refugee, or he could abandon his family and go off to fight. In either case his already poor family would be left destitute, so neither choice was a solution.

The farmer made regular visits to town and kept us informed about his situation. When several weeks passed and we did not hear from him, we began to fear that the worst had happened. Word of our concern reached him, and he came into town to assure us that he was all right. We were happy to learn that he was still alive and were overjoyed to see that he was a changed individual. As he talked with us, he calmly looked us straight in the eye. His hands were steady, and he spoke with quiet self-assurance. The farmer told us that while he was contemplating what he ought to do, a new choice presented itself to him. Somehow he came to the realization that he should not make any decisions solely out of fear. If he claimed to be a Christian—which he did—he ought to make his decisions based on faith. He expressed his insight in this way: "If they come and kill me, well, that will be the end of me, and may God forgive them for it. They can kill me but I will not run away or join anyone just because I am afraid of what might happen to me."

Although the farmer still had the difficult task of deciding every day what was best for his family, he was able to make better and wiser decisions with his new faith than with his old fear. For the time being he chose neither to flee nor to fight. Instead, he remained on his land. The day he expected to be killed never came. He was able to work his fields for several years before a different set of circumstances made leaving his home the wiser course of action. Even then he acted as a man of faith and not fear. Quietly he moved his family to town and began to wait patiently for the day when he could return to his land.

Our farmer friend had what is called in Latin America a *lucha*. The Spanish word means a "struggle" or a "fight." The people use the word in a variety of contexts and in reference to the struggles for life, for peace, and for justice. They also use the word *lucha* when they talk about faith. For them, faith is a struggle. But that struggle is not, as we might think, over whether to live by faith or to live without it. The struggle is over whether faith or fear will rule in their lives.

The *lucha* between faith and fear is epitomized in the gospels by the conflict between Jesus and his antagonists. Jesus was a man of faith, obedient to his Father even in the face of death. Those who opposed Jesus, the religious and civil leaders of his time, are described as men of fear. Instead of having faith in God or in themselves, those men bowed to external pressures and their own timidity. For instance, the chief priests, Scribes, and Pharisees who sought to condemn Jesus were not the men of faith they claimed to be. Jesus exposed them as fear-driven men when he caught them in a trap they had set for him.[1] In an attempt to discredit Jesus, they questioned him concerning the source of his authority. Jesus said he would answer their question, but only after they answered an older question—the legitimacy of John's Baptism. As religious leaders, they had the responsibility of giving instruction and direction to the Jewish community on matters of faith. With regard to John's Baptism, they had given no guidance to their people about what to believe. Because they were afraid, they had not spoken. They would not say that John's Baptism was not from God, because they feared the people's faith in the prophet. Nor would they say that John's Baptism was from God, which would have revealed their religious duplicity in not accepting it themselves. Forsaking their sacred duty of leading the people in faith, these religious leaders took the coward's way out and pleaded ignorance. Because of their fear, those who attempted to discredit Jesus were themselves discredited. Ironically, what they most feared most of all, namely, faith in Jesus, was what they needed most of all.[2]

In matters of faith and fear, Jesus was as much of a challenge to the civil rulers of his day as he was to the religious leaders. When King Herod heard about Jesus, the Word of God that came to him through John the Baptizer judged him.[3] Herod had been both disturbed by the Baptist's words and attracted to what John had to say. Although Herod had listened attentively to John for hours, he could not bring himself to accept John's message, because Herod was a man of fear. He had feared John as a just and holy man; he also feared the Baptist's followers, who regarded their spiritual leader as a prophet.[4] Herod had even ordered John's execution because of fear. Herod was a prime example of a person who lost the struggle for faith. He had made a throne for fear in his heart. Herod's reaction to the stories about Jesus showed his fear once again. Getting rid of John had not eliminated that fear.

Pontius Pilate was another frightened individual who stood before Jesus.[5] Although Pilate could find no case against Jesus, his fear dissuaded him from passing a just judgment. Pilate feared the mob and what might be said to his superiors about him. Instead of acting in the manner of a noble Roman, Pilate responded as a coward and handed Jesus over to be crucified.

Everywhere in the gospels, Jesus' faith is sharply contrasted to the fear of his adversaries. While his enemies were afraid to speak the truth, Jesus never stopped proclaiming it. Unlike his antagonists, Jesus was recognized as a person who did not court anyone's favor or "act out of human respect;" Jesus was afraid of no one.[6] The Son of God considered fear to be useless.[7] Anyone who would act out of fear was as worthless as the servant in the Parable of the Talents.[8] Entrusted with some of the king's wealth, the servant was too frightened of the ruler to do anything with the money except bury it in the ground. Actually, the king was quite reasonable in expecting some return for his money. He said that he would have been satisfied with the interest it would have earned if put out on loans. Fear of the ruler, however, had blinded the servant to the king's true character and to the simple solution to his dilemma of how to safeguard the money. Following the dictates of his fear, the servant acted foolishly and ended up suffering what he hoped to avoid. Because of his fear, the servant was of no use to the king, who banished him from his sight. The servant was salt that had lost its flavor, good for nothing but to be thrown out and trampled underfoot.[9]

Like the frightened servant of Jesus' parable, we too are of little value to Christ and his Kingdom if we allow fear to rule us. Except for those occasions when fear arises because of obvious physical danger, it is a subtle and pervasive power in our lives. We may be influenced for years by fears we do not know we have. We might think that we are living rationally and wisely, when all along we are merely following the promptings of our fears. Unless we seriously reflect upon what inspires our decisions and motivates our actions, we will not recognize many of our fears, and being aware of our fears is essential to overcoming them. Being unafraid does not mean that we never feel frightened. We are unafraid when, being able to name our fears, we do not allow them to be the deciding factor in the judgments we make and the actions we take.

In our struggle to be less fearful and more faithful, we often meet with discouragement when our faith does not seem to be what we think it should be. A search of the scriptures for step-by-step instructions on how to minimize our fear and increase our faith will not bring us much satisfaction either. Concerning fear, the gospels simply tell us not to have it: "Do not be afraid of anything;"[10] "Do not be afraid of those who kill the body and can do no more."[11] Concerning faith they simply tell us to have it: "Have faith in God and faith in [Jesus Christ]."[12] Even when the disciples specifically ask Jesus to increase their faith, he neither makes it grow for them nor offers them tips on how to gain faith themselves. He speaks to them only about what they could do if they had the least bit of faith.[13]

The gospels cannot tell us much about acquiring faith because faith is a mystery, and a mystery is an all or nothing proposition. It cannot be divided up or broken down into parts, like a journey that can be undertaken a step at a time. Passing from fear to faith is like moving from one train to another while they are on parallel tracks but going in opposite directions. As the trains pass each other, there is no slow or gradual way by which we can get from one to the other. To make the transfer, much more than a cautious step is needed. We must boldly jump from one to the other. That leap from a life dominated by fear to one dominated by faith changes our whole direction and puts us on the right track to the Kingdom.

Besides being a mystery, faith is also a gift God readily gives us. Although we cannot earn faith, there are things we can do to prepare ourselves to receive it. Above all, we can pray. Prayer is itself an act of faith and is most helpful in combatting fear. Our authority on the positive connection between prayer and faith is, of course, Jesus. He prayed that the faith of his disciples would never fail,[14] and when he himself was fearful, he left his companions to pray alone to his Father.[15]

Another way of preparing ourselves for an increase of faith is by allowing the Word of God to have power over us as it does over nature. In Mark's account of the storm on the lake, a word from Jesus calms the winds and waves of a raging sea.[16] Jesus speaks his command, "Peace, be still," not only to the elements of nature but to us as well. If we listen to our Lord instead of the fear in our hearts, we will marvel more at the tranquility Christ can effect in us than at the calm he can demand of nature. Sometimes in order that we might hear the Word of God more clearly, we must repeat it to ourselves. Peace, be still. Peace, be still. Peace, be still. Even though it may seem that we are only talking to ourselves, the Word of God bears repeating. By repeating Christ's words to ourselves, we are allowing our Lord to speak to us. Through listening to God in this way, it is not long before the Word settles into our hearts, where it uproots our fears and establishes faith and peace.

The faith of our farmer friend was remarkable and, in many ways, unmatchable. Fortunately, we do not have to compare our faith with his or think that we are alone in our struggle with fear. Whether we live in a Central American jungle or an asphalt one, whether we are accustomed to the noise of gunfire or industrial machinery, whether we know the heat from a tropic sun or from a boss's scrutiny, we all face the same fight. That we will succeed in our struggle, our *lucha*, for faith we should not doubt. The spirit that God has given to us is not a cowardly spirit, but the spirit of faith, a spirit "that makes us strong, loving and wise."[17]

The Called

I first met Sister Dorothy Kazel, O.S.U. at San Salvador's old international airport in January of 1980. She was there with others of the Cleveland Diocesan Mission Team to welcome me to El Salvador. As I got off the plane and walked across the tarmac to the terminal, I saw Dorothy smiling and waving enthusiastically from the observation deck. I was nervous about coming to El Salvador, but upon seeing that my arrival meant something to her and the rest of the team, I temporarily regained some self-confidence. While I was waiting in line for the customs inspection, however, I grew apprehensive again. Everything that had seemed new and exciting about being a missionary was suddenly strange and frightening. I glumly pondered what I had gotten myself into by volunteering to work in El Salvador. In an effort to take my mind off my worries, I looked around and saw Dorothy watching me from the waiting area. She was following my progress through the entrance procedures with keen interest. She waved at me then and every time I looked in her direction. It was as if she knew what I was feeling and was trying to reassure me from where she stood. She also gave me the impression that if I ran into any trouble, help was not far away. For that bit of communication, I was very grateful.

I do not know exactly how Dorothy did it, but when finally we were close enough to shake hands, she made our first meeting feel like a reunion of old friends. I can remember thinking that if a person whom I had never met could have such a good effect upon me, I should try to do the same for oth-

> ers. That a quiet and retiring person like me should even think about acting in such a manner, much less attempt a change in behaviour, was no small tribute to Dorothy and her exuberant example.
>
> Dorothy wanted to have that kind of effect on people, but not for any vain or selfish reason. She desired with all her heart to let her light shine before men and women so that in seeing her good works they would give honor and glory to God. In her own words, she wanted to be "a living alleluia."
>
> As conditions in El Salvador worsened, Dorothy's alleluia of hope and joy shone all the more brightly. It was not fearlessness, however, that made Dorothy a source of strength for us all. In those terrible times she was as frightened as the rest of us. It was what Dorothy did with her fear that kept her an alleluia from head to foot. With trust in her Lord, she found security in God and accepted fear as a part of her vocation of working among the poor. Dorothy taught us to do the same by leading us frequently in raising our hearts and voices in song to God.
>
> Dorothy's favorite song in El Salvador typified what she believed about meeting fear with faith in God. The song was entitled "Be Not Afraid." She sang it often and it was the last song she sang with us before she was murdered on December 2, 1980.

Along with every vocation there is an element of fear. This is true whether God's call is to a vocation in the traditional sense (priesthood, matrimony, religious life, single life) or to a vocation within a vocation, such as the call Sister Dorothy Kazel, an Ursuline nun from Cleveland, heard to serve the poor in El Salvador. That fear should accompany vocations is accepted in the gospels as part of God's call. Mary, Joseph, the disciples, and others were first introduced to their special vocations not with words like "Come, follow me," but with such words as "Do not be afraid" and "Have no fear." Before Mary heard of God's plan for her to bear a son named Jesus, she was greeted by the angel with the words, "Do not fear."[1] While Joseph pondered what to do with his betrothed who was pregnant, God told him through a dream to have no fear about taking Mary as his wife.[2] When Jesus spoke to Peter about catching men instead of fish, he urged him not to be afraid of trading an occupation for a vocation.[3] In calling his flock to discipleship, Jesus first invited the men he had chosen not to live in fear.[4]

Because accepting a vocation from God launches us into the unknown, it is only natural that we will experience some fear. When we answer a call from God, we do not know everything that will be asked of us. We do not know what awaits us in the future or where God will lead us. We do not know what joys will be ours or what pain we will suffer for the sake of the Kingdom. We do not know what God plans to accomplish through us or how God will do it. When we accept a vocation, we do not even know if we will be able to fulfill the task God has set for us.

Unless we find our security in God, through faith, fear will keep us from our vocation. If we allow our fear to control us, our lives will be without meaning and direction. Fear-filled, we will not only be indecisive, but also insignificant. The story of Zechariah in the first chapter of Luke's gospel is a figurative example of what happens to a person who, because of fear, does not answer God's call.

Zechariah was serving as priest in the sanctuary of the Lord when an angel appeared to him. Fear overcame Zechariah. The angel, however, exhorted him not to be afraid. God was calling him to participate in the plan of salvation by bearing witness to certain events that were about to take place in Israel. Afraid to believe God's Word, however, Zechariah lost the ability to speak. The silence that befell the priest was not the powerful silence by which we come to know, love, and serve God better. Nor was it that holy silence which speaks with authority and has much to say to a noise-gutted world. It was a barren silence out of which nothing could be said or accomplished. Speechless and impotent, Zechariah could only look on as God's plan to save his people unfolded without him. He who was to be a spokesman for God became a mute bystander when because of his fear he failed to believe God.

Like Zechariah, we too shall have nothing meaningful to say to anyone if we allow fear to choke off an affirmative response to God's call. We shall also be insignificant in God's plan of salvation if fear reigns in our heart rather than the Lord. Only by renouncing fear, as Zechariah later did when he indicated that his newborn son was to be named John, will we be able to give witness to God's marvelous deeds. Accepting a vocation from God with faith will fill us, as it did the prophet Zechariah, with God's spirit of holiness and give us a voice to proclaim to the world the Lord's salvific action among his people.

In that same chapter of Luke's gospel, the Holy Spirit also came upon Mary and filled Elizabeth, Zechariah's wife. The Spirit's presence among God's people just before the birth of Jesus links vocation to the mystery of the Incarnation. Vocation is, so to speak, an incarnation in reverse. By incarnation, the Son of God was "in-fleshed" in order to share in our life. By vocation we are "in-spirited," that is, filled or divinized by the Holy Spirit, so that we might share in the life of God. Through incarnation Jesus was sent by his Father into time and history to transform our world and bring it to its goal. Through vocation we are called through time and history to come to God and bring with us the fruits of our labors on earth. Incarnation was the unforeseeable and unexpected way God chose to come to us. Vocation is the unforeseeable and unexpected way God chooses for us to come to God.

In accepting and living a vocation from God, a canticle or song of faith can bolster our hearts when fear of the unknown or fear of trusting God's Word overtakes us. Zechariah has already given us his canticle, in which he reminds us that the Lord is powerful and calls us to serve him without fear, to be holy and just all of our days.[5] There are many other canticles from which we can choose. Sister Dorothy Kazel selected the song "Be Not Afraid" as her canticle of faith. It describes very well how she became the prophetic alleluia she wanted to be. By not being afraid to follow her Lord, Dorothy found in God her life, security, and rest. If we do not yet have a canticle of faith or a song of vocation we can make our own, I am sure that Dorothy would want to share hers with us.

Be Not Afraid

You shall cross the barren desert,
But you shall not die of thirst.
You shall wander far in safety
Though you do not know the way.
You shall speak your words in foreign lands and all
 will understand.
You shall see the face of God and live.

Be not afraid. I go before you always.
Come follow Me, and I will give you rest.

If you pass through raging waters in the sea,
You shall not drown.
If you walk amid the burning flames,
You shall not be harmed.
If you stand before the power of hell and death is
 at your side,
Know that I am with you through it all.

Be not afraid. I go before you always.
Come follow Me, and I will give you rest.

Blessed are your poor,
For the kingdom shall be theirs.
Blessed are you that weep and mourn,
For one day you shall laugh.
And if wicked men insult and hate you

All because of Me,
Blessed, blessed are you!

Be not afraid. I go before you always.
Come follow Me, and I will give you rest.

The Martyr

While Jean Donovan was in El Salvador, she saved the lives of a number of people. I am very familiar with the story of one of her rescues, because the life she saved was mine. On that occasion, no great heroics were involved. Courage alone would not have saved me. My life simply depended upon someone else's faith. Because of her faith and for no other reason, Jean was present at the moment I desperately needed help.

Jean saved my life during a period when our mission team was keeping only a skeleton crew in the country. Archbishop Romero had just been murdered, and no one knew what was going to happen next. Curtailing our presence in the area was thought to be the prudent course of action. During that time, Jean was working at our mission located near the capital. On two separate occasions, once with Sister Dorothy Kazel and once by herself, Jean made the three-hour, cross-country trip to our rural mission, where I was working alone. On her second visit, Jean and I were eating dinner when I began to choke on a piece of chicken. The food blocked all air to my lungs. Gagging convulsively, I knew I was going to die if I did not get the obstruction out of my throat. But despite all my efforts, I could not dislodge it. As I faced the likely prospect that my life was at an end, a hundred and one thoughts crossed my mind. Not all of those thoughts, however, were the kind I had presumed people had during the last moments of life. For instance, I can remember thinking how embarrassed I was going to be if I died. So many people were being killed by bullets and bombs that it seemed as though violent death was the normal way to die in that country. With everyone hoping to escape death, but expecting a martyr's end, I wondered how I would ever live it down when word got out that I died in El Salvador choking on a piece of chicken!

As these thoughts and recollections occupied my brain, the clear picture of where I was and what I was doing started to get fuzzy around the edges. Just as I was losing touch with my surroundings, I was struck on the back by a blow that seemed to come out of nowhere. The next thing I knew, I was holding that tough piece of chicken in my hand and was breathing again. I sat quietly for a moment, enjoyed the pleasure of being able to breathe, and tried to understand what had happened. I looked over my shoulder in the direction that the blow had come from and there was Jean, standing behind me and getting ready to hit me again. So as not to be on the receiving end of another blow, I quickly assured her that I was all right.

As Jean returned to her chair, I was hit again, but not by my dining partner. I was struck by the thought of what would have happened if Jean had not been there. Jean had come that afternoon and was leaving the next day. Except for Dorothy and Jean's two visits, I had eaten alone every evening for the past month. If I had swallowed wrong on any of those nights, I would have choked to death. I could think of only one reason why Jean Donovan was present to help me that night. It was not luck that she was there. Nor was it a coincidence. It had nothing to do with courage or strength. What brought her to our rural mission that day was the same thing that frequently put her in the right place at the right time to give the assistance that was needed. It was her faith in God.

Jean's faith was unique. Because of it she allowed God to direct her to people and places. By her faith, she also gave witness to the homeless, the hungry, the sick, and the imprisoned concerning the presence of God among them. If Jean had lived at the time of the early Church, she would have been called a martyr of the faith even while she lived. In the ancient world a martyr was a witness who by word or deed gave testimony to the truth. The early Christians appropriately considered themselves martyrs, that is, witnesses of the Good News.[1] By what they said and did they testified to the power that Jesus' saving actions had in their lives. Whether their earthly existence ended violently in a pool of blood at an arena or peacefully in bed at home mattered little to them. What was more important was to have given faithful witness to Christ's presence in life as well as in death.

Identifying themselves as martyrs, the early Christians understood their vocation from God as a call to a lifelong martyrdom. What marked their vocation as that of a martyr was not one death, but many deaths. Before knowing Christ they had thought that in order to have life, they had to engage in a life-and-death struggle for it. There was but one death, and all their energies went to preserve themselves from it as long as possible. After seeing the light of Christ, they came to understand that saving themselves did not bring them life. Life was not a life-and-death struggle that they could never win, but a death-and-life experience that they were to enter into with faith. Being faithful to Christ was the only way to have life, even though at times it meant embracing a death experience. In accepting Christ as their saviour, they lived by a new law that might well be called "the martyr's code": "Whoever would preserve his life will lose it, but whoever loses his life for my sake and the gospel's will preserve it."[2] According to scripture, the first Christians recognized that death could be experienced in many different ways. They were to have faith in God, not just at the time of physical death, but whenever they felt as though they were dying. By believing in Jesus as he believed in his Father, they were to be witnesses to the Good News that in every kind of death experience, the possibility for life remained. They would share in Christ's life if they suffered those deaths in his name.

Of course, to lose one's life in order to preserve it was always easier said than done. It was as difficult to recognize and achieve an act of martyrdom as it was to recognize and believe in Jesus. Strong human emotions nearly always focused attention upon death rather than life. Because Mary Magdalene did not yet believe in the death-and-life miracle of resurrection, she thought the only explanation for the disappearance of Jesus' body from the tomb was that it had been stolen. Her grief was so blinding that she mistook the Risen Lord for a gardener.[3] Likewise the disheartened disciples on the road to Emmaus did not recognize Christ, even though they spent the better part of an afternoon with him.[4] In their discouragement they had believed that Jesus' life had ended in death and not as the scriptures and Jesus himself had foretold. Human emotions and feelings did not lead the disciples to the mystery that would bring them their greatest joy. The confidence that out of death God could and did bring life came to them only through faith in his Son.

Our emotions can distort our perception of a situation and can prevent us from recognizing Christ. Nevertheless we can use the feelings we associate with death to alert ourselves to opportunities to lose our lives for the sake of the Gospel. For example, when we use words such as "killing," "suffocating," "strangling," and "stifling" to describe the feelings we have in a certain situation, we can be reasonably sure that we are facing a moment in which we either choose or reject the way of the martyr. If we follow our instincts for self-preservation, we feel that our best chances for survival depend on our ability to keep ourselves out of harm's way. If we cannot escape personal injury, we want to put up a fight. When struck, we want to strike back; when hurt, we want to cause hurt. While it may seem that the only way to save ourselves is to defend ourselves, the martyr's code points out another way. Every experience in which we feel pain and suffering is an opportunity for giving a faithful witness to the saving power of Christ's love. In situations that are "killing" us, faith requires us to exercise forgiveness, kindness, generosity, or one of the other Christian virtues. Whatever it is that we must do in order to be faithful to Christ, God promises us that what we do in his name will not kill us. We shall have life, not death, by living as Christ did.

Our natural distaste for anything that feels like death makes us hesitate to embrace a lifetime of martyrdom. Yet we need not fear death in any of its forms, for we have already encountered death and have lived to tell about it. Yes, we have already died once, in baptism. But because we died with Christ, we have also risen to a new life with him. Martyrdom for the sake of the Kingdom allows us to draw continually on the life of Christ. Martyrdom preserves us from all forms of self-pity, and it does not leave us crotchety, cranky, or cross with others. Although what we might suffer in order to be authentic martyrs is painful, martyrdom mysteriously brings us joy. As martyrs who proclaim the presence of Christ in the world, we realize that there is nowhere to go for the words of life except to him. Being led where we might not want to go, but trusting God always to lead us, we no longer worry about what we are to say or do. Our hearts are gladdened when we realize that he can move us to be at the right place at the right time for someone else's benefit. Through his Spirit, our words and actions take on a new power to inspire and console others. Even though people tell us with increasing frequency that they are touched by what we say and do, no one has to tell us who the source of that goodness is. We know. And we rejoice and give thanks to God for seeing fit to incorporate us into salvific work.

Even if it should seem that God has chosen not to work miracles through us, we are not disturbed. We are, above all, martyrs, witnesses to God's power. We are happy to direct the attention of others to where God is and how God is working among us. If God should choose others to accomplish the work of the kingdom, we are not jealous or envious of them, for we are not in competition with them for God's favors and affection. As martyrs we rejoice wholeheartedly when he fulfills his purpose through the goodness of others. As martyrs we are content to testify about the wonderful things the Lord has done for his people. We can do all this because no one can take from us our greatest joy—the joy of being with Christ in death and in life.

Whether we chose the ancient or present-day meaning of the word "martyr" to describe Jean Donovan, she would have been the last person on earth to admit she was one. But Jean was truly a martyr, both before and after her death in December of 1980. Jean's friends recognized her desire and need to witness to the world concerning God's love. With a joviality that did not hide their admiration for Jean and the calling she accepted from God, they gave her a specially made T-shirt to wear in El Salvador. On it was printed "St. Jean, The Playful." Jean, always ready for a party, was the life of many a *fiesta*. While she never missed the opportunity for a celebration, she had traded a life devoted to fun and good times for the martyrdom of working with the poor. In the exchange she chose the better part; and the life she found in Christ she imparted to others, as well. Because she was a martyr in life, she was there with us and the poor in El Salvador when we needed her and her witness. Now in death, the world has her faithful witness that life is where she and every martyr in heaven and earth are—with God.

The Soldier and the Insurgent

During the twilight of one of the last days in May, a solitary soldier was kneeling in our parish church. In the darkening interior of the building, he was an unusual study of a person at prayer. The tools of his profession contrasted sharply with his devout bearing. Like a vicious animal, a rifle clung to his back. Grenades dangled menacingly from their straps. His ammunition belt bristled with shells. While his weapons were a warning not to come near him, the intensity with which he prayed was an invitation to seek the peace that comes from God alone.

Two weeks later, I encountered someone who reminded me of the praying soldier. Oddly enough that other individual was an insurgent. I discovered him in a chapel in a remote part of our parish. When I first saw him, he too was kneeling. His eyes were closed peacefully; his hands were folded reverently. His posture overall was attentive but relaxed. Despite the large rifle that peered over his shoulder, he gave every appearance of a person who was in loving communication with God. By the way he prayed, he stirred within me the same desire for intimacy with God that his military counterpart had.

I met the soldier and the insurgent during my first year in El Salvador. I have not seen either of them since. For all I know they both may have been killed in the war. I remember them not only for how they prayed, but also for the conversations we had. Each of them engaged me in a dialogue, but not about topics that would have concerned most soldiers and guerrillas. Neither talked about the

> war, politics, the Church, or the United States. Instead, one asked for sacramental forgiveness, the other, for priestly guidance in his relationship with God.
>
> Because I obviously did not know all the soldiers and insurgents who were involved in the fighting in El Salvador, I cannot make a general statement about their faith. I do know, however, that no matter which side the young men of that tiny country named after our Saviour fought for, each side had at least one man of faith in its ranks. And where one man of faith can be found, there undoubtedly are more.

From the teachings of Jesus Christ we have always known that faith is not the exclusive possession of any one people or nation. Every age and place has its soldier and its insurgent, that is, persons who are diametrically opposed to each other by conviction but who are both motivated by a living and vibrant faith. If we have never met two such individuals, the gospel gives us that opportunity by introducing us to the soldier and the insurgent of Jesus' day. The soldier was the Roman centurion whose servant Jesus cured;[1] the insurgent was the criminal who died on a cross alongside of Jesus.[2]

The Roman centurion represented everything that was abhorrent to the Jewish community to which Jesus preached. The centurion was a gentile, a pagan, a foreigner, a visible reminder of the conqueror, and an enforcer of the hated Roman laws and taxes. By the direct orders of men like him, the feared Roman legions were sent into battle, uprisings were put down, and Jewish citizens were executed. To imagine that a centurion could be a man of faith was unthinkable for those who were oppressed by these professional soldiers. To declare, as Jesus did, that a Roman centurion had more faith than any Israelite was to turn the world of religious belief upside down.

The praise the centurion received from Jesus for his faith was well deserved. At a time when many were asking the man of Nazareth to work signs and wonders so that they might believe in him, the soldier made no such request. The centurion already believed in Jesus as one who had authority over life. Because the centurion was familiar with authority, he knew that Jesus need not visit his home in order to cure his servant; a word from Jesus was all that was necessary. Having received that word, the centurion immediately started his homeward journey. By promptly assuming that the deed had been done, the Roman centurion, a soldier of Caesar and a defender of pagan gods, showed that he was inspired and animated by his faith in Jesus Christ.

The insurgent's counterpart was the man who was crucified at Jesus' right side. The scriptures identify that man as a robber, a criminal,[3] and an insurgent.[4] Amidst the turmoil in Palestine at that time, the man could have been any or all of these. Wherever there were insurrections and revolts it was, as always, difficult to determine a person's motivation for engaging in a violent struggle. As armed conflict polarized the country, one man's heroism became another man's treason—one man's virtue, another man's crime. A group of men known as Zealots, for instance, had dedicated themselves to freeing their homeland of foreign domination. Enjoying a certain amount of popular support, they stirred up public sentiment against the Romans. Whenever it was feasible, the Zealots waged guerrilla wars against them. In the eyes of the Zealots, nothing good came from Rome, and all Romans were tyrants and oppressors. The Romans, on the other hand, did not recognize the Zealots as a political group. Even though the Zealots saw themselves as liberators fighting for the holy cause of justice, the Romans referred to them as bandits. According to the Roman way of thinking, there was no reason to distinguish between the Zealots and the bands of robbers and murderous thieves that terrorized the countryside. Since every one of them disrupted public order and broke civil laws, the Romans considered them all to be criminals deserving the same treatment—crucifixion. In a climate that bred blind hatred, not even someone like Jesus could escape condemnation. He who was innocent of all wrongdoing was found guilty of being a subversive and sentenced to die for trying to force the collapse of the nation.[5]

Whether the man who was crucified with Jesus was a robber, a criminal, or an insurgent can never be determined. But certainly the man's crimes consisted of more than theft. Generally, the Romans were not in the habit of crucifying petty thieves. They reserved that punishment for those whom they held in utter contempt, such as insurrectionists and revolutionaries. And this condemned man himself did not think he was being treated unjustly; he acknowledged the serious nature of his crimes when he admitted that he deserved to die for what he had done.[6]

That man, however, was a "good thief" in this sense: he recognized his chance to steal for himself a place in the kingdom and he took it. He snatched a priceless treasure and got away with it because of his faith in Jesus. More than anything else, it was the man's faith that counted with our Lord. Like the centurion, the good thief had a faith that did not depend upon miracles. Unlike the bystanders who watched the executions on Calvary and protested that only Jesus' descent from the cross could make believers out of them,[7] the good thief had already placed his faith in Jesus of Nazareth. Even though Jesus did not rescue him from his cross, the good criminal believed in Jesus, the son of a carpenter. Even though the beaten and bloody man next to him did not look like the ruler of a powerful kingdom, the good insurgent believed in Jesus, the King of the Jews. Whoever it was that died at the right side of Jesus, he was a man of faith.

Faith is what matters to Christ. Because of faith he can accept into his kingdom persons with such diverse backgrounds and purposes as the centurion and the insurgent. Christ looks past a person's clothes, creeds, causes, and character into the individual's heart. There he seeks a faith that expresses itself as a willingness to accept the Good News and follow him.

While Christ can look into the heart of an individual and see the faith there, we do not always see in others what he does. Appearances can deceive us. Because faith is often hidden from view, those whom we consider the farthest from God may enter the Kingdom ahead of the religious and pious.[8] Because we are unable to measure anothers' faith, the Day of Judgment will be for us a time when one person is taken into heaven while another is left behind, even though both are engaged in exactly the same activity.[9] Under certain circumstances we may be required for the good of the community, to judge another person's *actions,* but as to the ultimate character of an individual *person,* we may never pass judgment. Lacking divine insight, we do best when we heed God's warning not to judge others.[10]

Although our neighbor's faith is hidden from us, our own faith in Christ and his Kingdom reveals to us the truth about others. Concerning the truth, Jesus told Pilate that his Kingdom was completely devoid of any political or national dimensions.[11] His Kingdom did not have the divisions that are in every earthly kingdom. As the Apostle Paul would later write about the Kingdom, there is no distinction between Gentile and Jew, circumcised and uncircumcised, male and female, slave and freeman. All are one in Christ Jesus.[12] Even before Pilate could ask his famous question, "What is truth?" Jesus had already answered it. The truth was that every member of the human race was brother or sister to every other member and he, Jesus, was the Lord of all. Because Pilate was not committed to the truth, however, he neither heard nor accepted Jesus' invitation to have faith in his Kingdom. Pilate insisted on political and national divisions. He demanded that distinctions between people be made. He, for instance, was quick to point out that he was not a Jew, he was a Roman and he believed that such differences were too great for any kingdom to overcome.

To be sure, Jesus knows the hearts of men and women.[13] He knows that not everyone will accept a Kingdom in which all are one in him. Like Pilate, who washed his hands of Jesus, many will wash their hands of the truth. They will persist as Pilate did in believing that the world is a place divided between "us" and "them" and that life is a struggle carried on between the "good guys" and the "bad guys." Rather than jeopardize the existing order, they will prefer to eliminate anyone who offers serious opposition to their views. Therefore, Jesus warns those of us who preach his Kingdom that we will be persecuted for telling the truth just as he was.[14]

Someday we will witness the truth for ourselves. When we discover among the ranks of the saints in heaven a Salvadoran soldier standing next to a Salvadoran insurgent, we will not be surprised. The precedent was set long ago by Jesus when he welcomed into his Kingdom a Roman centurion and a Jewish insurgent. Like those two, the Salvadoran soldier and insurgent will not be there because of the causes for which they died, but because of the faith with which they lived. Their faith in God will be what has saved them from condemnation.[15] Moreover, we will recognize them not as soldier or insurgent, but as brothers of ours, for we will have arrived at the same state by precisely the same route. We will share in Christ's glory together, not because of anything we did to merit salvation, but because of the faith we had in a God who is Lord of all.

The Good

The mayor of our small town was a good man. Secundino was not like other public officials. He did not accept bribes, cheat the people, and work only to maintain his position of power. Secundino treated everyone fairly, had the best interest of the community at heart, and made the services of his office available even to those who could not pay for them. One of the greatest tributes to this man was that he had not campaigned for the office of mayor. The community-at-large asked him to accept the job.

Secundino had not always been an outstanding member of society. For many years he had been one of the annoying and troublesome drunks who lived in the town. However, through the encouragement of a parish priest, the help of Alcoholics Anonymous, and his own resolutions, Secundino brought about a change for the better in himself. He attended a special school for adults and increased his proficiency in reading and writing. He also received training in agriculture and leadership. Equipped with new skills, Secundino involved himself in the work of the church and unselfishly gave his time and talents to service projects that benefitted the whole community. Eventually he became a religious lay leader and helped to spread Christ's message throughout the region.

During the years that Secundino was experiencing this transformation, life in his country was also undergoing a change, but not for the better. Anyone who tried to work for the good of society was silenced by threats of death. People disappeared. Unidentifiable bodies were dumped along the roadsides at night. Teachers were killed. Labor organizers were killed. Catechists were killed. Doctors and nurses were killed. Priests and religious workers were killed. The school that Secundino had attended, along with several other institutions like it, was forced to close. Programs that taught the *campesinos* (poor farm laborers and peasants) to read and write, to sign their names, and to know their rights under the existing laws of the land were called "subversive activities," inspired by communists. In the face of open persecution and a reign of terror, fewer and fewer men could be counted on to govern the people justly. When the townspeople asked Secundino to be their mayor, he was reluctant to take the position. As mayor he could accomplish much good, but he would also be in great danger. After lengthy and prayerful deliberation, he accepted the office. Secundino took his responsibilities seriously. He proceeded to make his administration one which served the good of the community and permitted the poor of the district to find justice.

Certain men, however, hated Secundino. They could not tolerate the presence of a good man. Secretly they decreed that he should die. On a bright June morning Secundino spent the last moment of his life on earth facing the wall of his office while a death squad shot him in the back.

In this world, evil often occurs in the midst of great beauty. Besides our mayor, thousands of men, women, and children have been brutally slain in the loveliest of the Central American countries. El Salvador's tropical weather, sunny skies, sandy beaches, and towering volcanoes made it a tourist's delight in the years before the violence erupted. The country's flowering plants and trees and its variety of familiar and exotic fruits such as bananas, coconuts, grapefruits, guayavas, mangos, oranges, papayas, and pineapples gave visitors the impression that they were vacationing in a lush garden. Yet since the outbreak of widespread violence, neither native nor foreigner has been able to enjoy the natural splendor of that tropical paradise. Against the beautiful panorama of El Salvador, the war exposed the diabolical nature of evil for what it really is: that which keeps us from experiencing goodness and beauty.

Scripture tells us that since the beginning of the human race, evil's purpose has been to separate us from all that is fine and good. According to the third chapter of the book of Genesis, evil lured Adam and Eve away from the goodness of God with a promise of power. Evil promised them the power of knowing good and evil if they ate the fruit God forbade them to touch. The attraction this temptation held for Adam and Eve was its appeal to their human reason. Herein lay evil's cunning. A temptation that asked Adam and Eve to turn against God outright would not have succeeded. Adam and Eve were created good. They were attracted naturally to what was good. They would not have done anything so obviously evil as to defy God openly. In order to be a temptation for Adam and Eve, consuming the forbidden fruit had to make sense to them. It had to appear to them that eating the fruit was the reasonable thing to do and that some good would come of it. Towards this end, evil presented the fruit as good in itself. The fruit was pleasing to the eye and looked as if it would be good for food. Evil also gave a good reason for eating it. Evil said that the fruit was desirable for the knowledge of good and evil it could impart. Any person who possessed that knowledge would be as good as God.

Convinced that eating the fruit would be good for them, Adam and Eve bit into it, even though their decision meant disobeying God's explicit instructions. Rather than trust in God to tell them what was good, they chose to rely on reason without faith. In denying who they were by repudiating their need for faith they became the first human beings to bite off more than they could chew.

Evil's promise of knowing good and evil was not an entirely empty one. Adam and Eve did acquire some knowledge. Yet that knowledge came tragically, through the bitter taste of evil itself in the sadness of separation from God. In allowing themselves to be seduced by evil, they divorced themselves from the source of life. Even before they were driven from the garden, they could no longer enjoy, as they once had, its goodness and beauty.

It is not a coincidence in the Scriptures that the temptation of Jesus in the desert[1] resembles the temptation of Adam and Eve in the garden. Although bread, kingdoms, and a temple were used instead of fruit, evil took the same approach with Jesus, the New Adam and Eve, as it had with the first Adam and Eve. Evil appealed to Jesus' reason and his human desire to do what was good. Changing stones into bread would diminish hunger. Removing earthly kingdoms from the dominion of evil and putting them under the reign of Christ would benefit all who lived in them. Demonstrating in a dramatic way that Jesus was in the care of the angels would lead people to know and love God. The temptations to do what appeared to be undeniably good were compelling. Jesus, however, refused to do what those temptations suggested, but not because he wanted the hungry to be without bread, nations without peace, and the human family without a common belief in God. Jesus spurned the opportunity to exercise natural, political, and religious power at the behest of evil because it meant breaking faith with his Father. No good would ever come from such a loss of faith. No kingdom would ever stand for very long without faith. Evil knew God's intent and knew that Jesus Christ had not come to establish a kingdom based on public displays of power. If evil desired an ultimate victory over goodness, it had to tempt Jesus into building his Kingdom in any way other than with faith.

From the historical perspective we now have, we ought to be able to see for ourselves the importance of faith. For the most part we presently have at our disposal the powers evil tempted Jesus to use in his day. We have the technology and resources to turn deserts into farmland and thereby put bread on every table. We have communication systems that provide us with the means to settle differences between the nations of the world and to create global peace. With the push of a button, our televisions and radios show us our brothers and sisters across the world, reveal their dreams and hopes, joys and sorrows, and remind us we would all be better off if we allowed our belief in the same loving and merciful God to unite us. In short, we have all the power necessary to satisfy world hunger, establish worldwide peace, and unite ourselves through a common belief in the one true God. What keeps us from using this power is what Jesus seeks to bring us by establishing his Kingdom: faith in God and in each other.

In the desert, evil failed to entice Jesus into acting without faith. Evil recognized its defeat and departed, but only for awhile. During Jesus' passion, evil returned and tried to coerce him into abandoning the will of his Father. The temptations that Jesus suffered during his Passion were reminiscent of those he was subjected to in the wilderness. On his way to death on a cross, Jesus was tempted to save himself,[2] just as he had been tempted to save himself in the wilderness by changing stones into bread. Jesus was tempted to summon angels to rescue him,[3] just as he had been tempted to rely on God's angels to catch him if he jumped from the temple. Jesus was tempted to come down from the cross and be the people's Messiah,[4] just as he had been tempted to take dominion over all the people in the earthly kingdoms. In a diabolical twist, evil had taken some of the powers it had tried to seduce Jesus into using in the desert and victimized him with them in his passion. The religious and political powers that evil wanted Jesus to exercise at the beginning of his public ministry were used against him at the end of his life to condemn[5] him and sentence him to death.[6]

Evil's objective in using its powers to mock, torture, and kill Jesus was the same as in the desert: move Jesus to act with any power other than faith. Jesus might rescue himself from the hands of his tormentors or answer his critics with incontrovertible proof of his divinity; it did not matter to evil. Evil would welcome any show of power by Jesus so long as it was not a manifestation of the power of faith.

Jesus had many good reasons during his passion to abandon faith. But, unlike Adam and Eve, Jesus did not give in to the temptations he faced. To meet a sword with a sword or to strike a blow in return for every blow received was simply to replace one power with another power similar in nature. Christ did not come to be the strongest among us by that kind of power. He came in the spirit of faith, that we might draw life once again from the goodness of God. By responding to temptation with faith and not power, Jesus was true to himself and to the mission which his Father had given him.

From the temptations of Adam and Eve and the temptations of Jesus, we learn something about evil and about ourselves. We learn that evil has an awesome ability to make abandoning faith in God appear reasonable, logical, and good. About ourselves we learn that our very attraction to what is good makes us vulnerable to evil's attempts to separate us from God. We are easily seduced into thinking that we are sensible and reasonable enough to know a good thing when see it. In situations when we doubt God's concern, we are tempted to disregard what faith tells us is good for us. At such times we are tempted to forsake our faith in favor of reason alone.

The temptation to rely more on reason than on faith is strong, particularly when we experience injustice. Injustice offends our belief in God, whether we are its victim or someone else's. We wonder why God permits it, why evildoers go unpunished, and why the wicked prosper by their deeds. When our sense of justice is outraged, evil tempts us to respond to the injustices not with reason and faith, as we should, but with reason and whatever power is available. The consequences of giving into this temptation are often worse than the injustices we try to correct.

Serious accidents and tragedies can also be moments of great temptation. Misfortunes cause us pain and test our faith, principally because there is no reason they should happen to us. We do not have a clue about why tragedy should befall us, but we have a hundred reasons why it should not (for example, We are too young. We are too old. We are too important. Others depend upon us. There has been a mistake. We are not ready. Too many things still need our attention. We have so much for which to live. Everything has just started to go our way.) Evil tempts us in time of tragedy to believe that God is unfeeling, cruel, and vengeful. Like the disciples who said, "Teacher, does it not matter to you that we are going to drown?",[7] we may also lose faith and believe that God does not care about us. We might even go so far as to believe that God derives some sort of pleasure from our destruction.

While our attraction to goodness may be a weakness when it comes to temptations, it is also a great strength. The more trust we have in God, the more we will be drawn to the goodness of living in faith. Faith lets us see that life is good and worth living. Faith empowers us with goodness. And it gives our life meaning and purpose. On the other hand, if we have little or no faith, we experience the world as our first parents did after they fell into sin. Our predominant feeling is one of being out of touch with God, with ourselves, with others, and with our surroundings. Without faith we do not enjoy life. We become tense, anxious, fearful, and lonely. We find it increasingly hard to face life and we have less and less control over everyday events. The powers we develop to solve our problems give us more reasons to fear than to feel secure, and the good we try to accomplish by relinquishing some or all of our trust in God does not last.

The good people in this world are those who will not be separated from the source of all goodness by a loss of faith. The good will attract evil's attention and wrath, for it cannot allow them to live untested, untried, and untempted. Some, like Christ, Secundino, and thousands of other good people, evil does not allow to live in this world at all. But Jesus Christ invites us not to fear evil or its temptations, persecutions, injustices, and death. As all-prevailing as evil might seem to be in this world, its days of dwelling here are numbered. Much yet remains to be suffered by the good, but Christ has overcome the power of evil in this world.[8] We shall share in Christ's victory and glory if, like him, we remain united to the good and just God through faith.

The Poor

The people of the fishing village in our parish had built a chapel close to the beach. One day in the middle of the rainy season, I was standing in its doorway when a woman approached and asked to speak to me before mass. Since she looked deeply troubled, I suggested that we step outside so the people in the chapel could not overhear us. In relative privacy she began to speak, and I to listen.

The story of the woman's suffering began three years before, on the night several armed men came to her home. They dragged her nineteen-year-old son out of the house and killed him. Ever since that dark hour in her life, she had grieved, hated, and sworn revenge. Like most women in that village, she was poor. Even if she knew who her son's murderers were, she could never bring them to justice. As the months and years passed, her grief and hatred grew until she could no longer bear the pain they caused. All she wanted now was some peace.

Unfortunately the woman's story was all too familiar. I had heard it before, from many mothers. Where the other mothers left off in their stories, however, this woman was just beginning. She continued by telling me that her sorrow, anger, and desire for revenge had not brought her the consolation and the satisfaction she thought they would. Her suffering did not restore her son to her. Her pain did not bring her son's murderers to justice. She had tried everything in her power to achieve peace and justice. Everything, that was, except forgiveness. She had purposely avoided forgiving in favor of grieving and hating. At this time in her life, however, she had come to a remarkable conclu-

> sion—if she was to have the peace she sought, she would have to forgive the men who murdered her son. She was sure, she said, that whatever pain forgiving those men might cause, it could not be any greater than the suffering her sorrow and hatred had brought her.
>
> With the last statement, the woman finished what she had to say. For a long moment she just stood very still. It seemed she was summoning power that was hidden within her. Rain began to fall, but she did not notice. She slowly drew a deep breath and exhaled. When I saw tears trickle, then stream down her face, I knew what she had done. She had chosen to forgive her son's murderers! The little, serene smile that followed her tears told me that for the first time in three long years she knew peace.

To be poor is to be powerless. The poor have no control over what happens to them or their loved ones. They cannot fight back at the causes of their suffering. Like the woman whose son was murdered, the poor are defenseless when it comes to stopping the injustices perpetrated against them. They have nothing and, in the eyes of the world, are nothing. Yet God is fond of creating out of nothing. God chose to build the Kingdom the same way the creator made the universe.

Unlike other kingdoms, which subsist on tangible wealth and power, the Kingdom of God springs from the nothingness of poverty. God sent Jesus to preach a kingdom for the poor. To announce this Good News to the poor, Jesus came with nothing. He was born among the lowly. He had nowhere to lay his head. His throne was a wooden cross—his crown, a circlet of thorns. He established his Kingdom with only those powers that were available to the poorest of the poor. They were powers that everyone had at his or her disposal and that Jesus used while he was being nailed to a cross: faith in God the Father, hope in the resurrection, forgiveness of one's enemies, and love for all.

In choosing to build the Kingdom with the powers of faith, hope, love, and forgiveness, God blessed the poor. Because these powers are the only ones the poor have and the only ones by which a person can enter into the Kingdom, God's Kingdom belongs uniquely to the poor. No matter how impoverished or oppressed the poor are, no one can take the Kingdom from them. Even if the poor are denied every freedom and right, the Kingdom is always within their grasp.

The proclamation of a Kingdom of the poor, as we know, received neither immediate nor universal acceptance. The world does not consider the powers of God's Kingdom to be powers at all. Rather, the world perceives the Kingdom's powers of faith, hope, love, and forgiveness as signs of weakness and dismisses them as having little or no effect on global affairs. When someone publicly proposes them as the solution to our world, national, or personal problems, he or she is laughed at for being naive. Anyone who seriously lives by these powers alone usually ends up getting crucified in one way or another by the world.

The world's laughter at and intolerance of the Kingdom hide both disappointment and fear that can be traced back to the days of Jesus. Many of the people in Jesus' time had hoped that the Messiah would create a kingdom of instant peace and prosperity. When they saw that Jesus had pointed out the way of powerlessness as the road to his Kingdom, they were shocked. They had expected to receive salvation through the Lord's manifest power and glory and not through his suffering and death. Because Jesus' promise of life through death was unacceptable to many, it became a matter of utmost importance for the crowd at Jesus' execution to persuade him to come down from the cross. If Jesus would save himself by some means other than the way of the cross, they would not have to do what he did. They would not have to take up their crosses and follow him.[1] They would not have to trust themselves to God's mercy.[2] They would not have to die loving[3] and forgiving their enemies.[4]

Yet in order to have God's Kingdom of peace and justice, we

must do what Jesus did. We must embrace poverty, that is, powerlessness in this world. Indeed the poverty that Christ chose and that the Kingdom requires can be a stumbling block. Like the crowd that looked upon the crucified Jesus, we would prefer a miracle-working saviour to a poor one. Like the woman in the years before she forgave her son's murderers, we would rather search for other, easier, quicker, and more effective ways out of our suffering than the way of the cross. What we often do not realize, however, is that refusing to use the powers of God's Kingdom causes us more suffering than anything else. Whether we keep ourselves from the Kingdom by our fear of embracing poverty or by our lack of conviction that God's ways will work does not matter. Our separation from the Kingdom is the source of most of the pain we experience in life.

Like the woman who found peace in forgiving, we shall discover life in the gospel that is preached to the poor only if we become poor ourselves. Being poor for the sake of the Kingdom consists in this:

- Having faith in God at all times and in every situation;
- Trusting in God's promise of life, even though at the moment we see nothing in which to hope;
- Loving those who persecute and calumniate us, even though they refuse to love us in return and continue to do us harm;
- Forgiving those who have wronged us, even though they have no intention of asking pardon.

Although being as powerless as the poor and relying on those powers Jesus used while dying on the cross can be an obstacle for those of us who seek to enter the Kingdom of God, that stumbling block is also a threshold. Embracing poverty as Jesus did is the way into the Kingdom; being a part of the Kingdom is the way to life.

The Charitable

At any one time in our parish we knew a number of people who faced deplorable situations. During one particular week, for example, a paralytic lay wasting away in his own home because his family was incapable of caring for him. Poor diet, unsanitary conditions, bed sores, and lack of therapy debilitated him more than his infirmity. That same week three children came into town by themselves. Men they could not identify had killed their parents and two other members of the family. The orphans had no known relatives and were alone in the world. Almost as bereft, a family fleeing the fighting in the north wandered aimlessly around the village square. They had no place to go, no money and no hope. Nor were they the first refugees to come into the area. Hundreds had preceded them, and the land's capacity to accommodate them all was dwindling.

These were just a few of the people who sought help in our parish. As parish staff, we did what we could to assist them, but the greatest acts of charity were performed by the parishioners themselves. A man named Valeriano heard of the paralytic's plight. He knew that the invalid would be better off at his house, where a cleaner and more suitable environment offered him the chance to regain some of his health. Even though Valeriano had a large family to support and his own problems to solve, he took the man under his care. Two families who themselves lived in stick huts welcomed the three orphans into their homes and loved them as their own. The community-at-large made room for the refugee family from the north. Some people donat-

> ed corn and beans from their own meager supplies. Others gave them building material and assistance in erecting a shelter against the sun and rain.
>
> The remarkable charity we witnessed began when the people of our town saw another's poverty and asked themselves the question, "What ought we to do?" The charitable were not afraid to ask that question nor to answer it with generosity.

"What ought we to do?" This was the question the people asked John the Baptist.[1] The prophet had come out of the desert and called them to have faith in God, repent of their sins, and be baptized. Being a simple and practical people, they wanted to know in terms they could understand what having faith meant. So the people asked John, "What ought we to do?" John was ready for their question, and he answered it straightforwardly: "Let the man with two coats give to him who has none. The man who has food should do the same."[2] In other words, the change of heart John preached required that believers see the discrepancies between what they had and what others needed. If their repentance and conversations were genuine, their faith would compel them to meet the needs of their neighbors with generous amounts of charity.

Two groups of men who heard John's reply were the tax collectors and the soldiers. Because their roles in society differed from those of the ordinary citizen, they wanted to know if faith demanded anything special of them. John answered them, too, with startling clarity. Tax collectors were not to exact anything over and above the fixed rate. Soldiers were to treat the people fairly, not bullying them or falsely accusing them of wrongdoing. They were also to be content with their wages.[3] In this way, John told those entrusted with civil responsibilities to practice not only a private kind of charity, but also a public charity better known as justice.

The biblical example of a man who was charitable in both his private and public life is Zacchaeus.[4] A tax collector, Zacchaeus may have been present when his colleagues asked John about what they were to do. He may even have been the one who voiced the question. Whether he was actually there or had heard of John's preaching through others, Zacchaeus took the Baptist's words to heart when he met Jesus. As a private citizen, he gave half of all he had to the poor. As a tax collector he paid back with interest those he had defrauded. Jesus approved of Zacchaeus' charity and called him a son of Abraham. Because of Zacchaeus' generous behavior, Jesus assured him that salvation had come to his house.

The question that the people asked of John the Baptist also was asked of Jesus by a rich young man.[5] Jesus' reply, like John's, emphasized again the importance of charity. Although the youth had done well in keeping the commandments, he had not really accomplished much toward achieving eternal life because he was lacking charity. If the youth truly desired to share in God's glory, he would have to give his riches to the poor. Charity was "the one thing more" necessary for salvation. And yet, even if the young man divested himself of his luxuries, Jesus did not want him to consider charity the last step to sanctity. Charity was (and still is) the all-important and unavoidable first step to holiness. Jesus communicated the importance of charity to this young inquirer by inviting him to distribute his wealth to the needy and become one of his disciples.

By word and by deed, Jesus preached the need for charity in the life of the faithful. On the day reserved for worship and rest, Jesus cured the sick,[6] the crippled,[7] and the blind.[8] Jesus worked those miracles not only to heal physical maladies, but also spiritual blindness. Of the two, those afflicted with the latter were in greater need of healing. Disturbed by Jesus' behavior on the Sabbath, they could not see that charity followed upon faith. Therefore, a charitable act did not break the law that forbade labor on the holy day, but rather gave the Sabbath worship and rest their value and meaning. If God's people were not charitable, their faith was dead and all their religious observances were hypocrisy.

The necessity of being charitable in order to be holy is the underlying theme of the Parable of the Good Samaritan, also.[9] In that parable Jesus identified the two travelers who passed by the brutally beaten victim of a robbery as men of religion. Although the priest and Levite seemed callous towards the dying man, Jesus did not criticize them simply because they were hard-hearted. These were men who had grown up in a religious tradition that valued charity. They knew what the laws of charity demanded of them and were willing to fulfill those laws when they encountered a neighbor in need. They had difficulty, however, in recognizing who their neighbor was and when he or she needed help. What Jesus found fault with was their inclination to overrate the significance of their religious observances. The importance they attached to certain pious practices blinded them to their neighbor's needs.

One of the beliefs by which the priest and Levite lived forbade them to come into contact with a corpse. In the situation described in the parable, it was therefore extremely important for the priest and Levite to know if the man was alive or dead. Had it been apparent that the victim needed some assistance, they would have given it, especially since he was a Jew like themselves. But the man's condition was not obvious to them from where they stood on the other side of the road. Our own experiences in El Salvador proved to us how difficult it was to determine merely by looking at a body lying on the ground whether the person was dead or alive. On a number of occasions, people we thought to be dead were unconscious and alive. With proper care some of these were nursed back to health. But afraid even to approach the body lest they became unclean, the priest and Levite refused to check for vital signs. Instead, they drew their own conclusions about the injured man. Rather than jeopardize their ritual purity, they chose to disregard charity and to continue on their journey without lifting the finger that would have saved the man's life. It was for their decision to put pious practices before charity that they received Jesus' condemnation.

Under the delusion of religious piety, the priest and the Levite sought their own convenience in the question of what they ought to do with the dying man. A character in another of Jesus' parables did the same with his wealth.[10] Asking himself what he ought to do with his abundance of material goods, the rich man answered the question according to his own desires. Instead of thinking about who might benefit from his good fortune, he foolishly kept his riches for his own enjoyment.

The lessons of the Good Samaritan and Foolish Rich Man parables clarify what we ought to do, especially with respect to charity. Do we have a conflict between the observance of a religious practice and the need for charity, as the priest and the Levite did on the road to Jericho? Those whose faith is genuine give precedent to acting with charity. Must we, like the foolish rich man, choose between enjoying the fruits of our labors and generously distributing them among the poor? We must, and the wise person pursues the way of charity. What do we do when our feelings rebel against the idea of being kind to someone we hate? Those who love set aside their personal feelings in favor of works of charity, as did the good Samaritan when, despite the great animosity between their peoples, he showed compassion to the injured Jew.

If we are uncomfortable with the way our Lord describes charity, we should not be surprised. Charity, in its private, social, and public expressions, is the oldest and most revolutionary idea we can contemplate. Thomas Paine, who helped inspire our own American Revolution, wrote about the ancient and revolutionary nature of charity in this way: "It is wrong to say that God made rich and poor. He made only *male* and *female,* and He gave them the whole Earth for their inheritance."[11]

Charity and justice are ideals that are as old as God's plans for humankind. They are the most revolutionary of ideals as well, because they call not only for "turning around" governments and institutions, but also for a revolution in our own hearts. Only the charity of private citizens and the justice of public officials can assure that the inheritance divinely given to all is enjoyed by all. Nations and peoples that are charitable work to achieve such a goal. They share what they have with the poor, who have been denied their rightful inheritance. They gladly give to those in need, even though they know there will be no repayment. They expect nothing in return for their charity because what they do is right and just in and of itself.

John's instructions to the people, Jesus' conversations with Zacchaeus and the rich young man, the parable of the Good Samaritan, and the parable of the Foolish Rich Man all declare that charity is necessary for holiness in this life and salvation in the next. In light of these teachings, the most crucial question of life is "What ought we to do?" People of faith answer that question by giving charity and justice to all who are in need of them.

The Lovers

In mid-1980, *Time* magazine reported that Salvadoran security forces had shot to death three doctors and four nurses during a raid on a clandestine hospital in a major city of El Salvador.[1] Many though not all of the patients in that makeshift facility were leftists who opposed the way the country was being run. One of the patients who was gunned down was a baby.

At that time in El Salvador, the slightest suspicion of cooperation with the opposition was enough in the minds of some to warrant the killing of "collaborators" and their friends. Whether the suspicion was grounded in fact or conjecture did not matter. Those who ordered the murders considered it easier to shoot suspects than to try them in court. Furthermore, the cold-blooded killings served as warnings to others.

Whatever the political convictions of the slain doctors and nurses, they had known that their actions would condemn them as rebel sympathizers. Yet even if they disagreed with the proponents of revolution, neither their personal views nor their status as medical professionals would protect them. Those doctors and nurses knew that their lives were in danger the moment they touched a wounded rebel. Aware of the implications of their actions, they chose, nevertheless, to put the alleviation of human suffering before politics. They saw their patients not as threats to a government, but as wounded people in need of the medical attention they could give. Without promise of reward and at great risk to themselves, those doctors and nurses responded to cries for help from fellow human beings.

The actions of the seven Salvadoran doctors and nurses are the kind of responses to individual needs that the Lord will extol at the Last Judgment as examples of true love.[2] According to Jesus' description of that day of reckoning, the Lord will announce from his throne that those on his right have inherited a place in his Kingdom. Although he will suggest that they have merited recognition through their kindness to him, the elect will not remember seeing him in pain or comforting him in his suffering. The Lord will tell them that they indeed loved him even though they did not see him. Every time they fed the hungry, gave drink to the thirsty, clothed the naked, sheltered the homeless, or visited the sick and imprisoned, they showed their love for him.

After this dialogue with the just, the Lord will focus his attention upon those who will not enter heaven. At first there will seem to be some mistake. The unjust will protest that every time they recognized the Lord in need, they did respond with charity. They will say on their own behalf, "Lord, when did we see you hungry or thirsty or away from home, or naked or ill or in prison and not attend you in your needs?" Ironically the words they will offer in self-defense will be the words that condemn them. The tragic flaw in their love is that unless they saw God in others they did not act. Come the Day of Judgment, they will think that they have loved well. But God will not ask them the question they are prepared to answer. Concerning their love for him, the Lord will not inquire of them, "Did you ever see me and not attend me?" Rather he will ask, "Even though you did not see me, did you care for the poor and insignificant people in your life as you would have cared for me?" Those who cannot say that they did will not go with the just into everlasting life.

Love that waits to see the presence of God before it takes action to meet the needs of others is not the love of God, but a disguised love of self. Besides missing many occasions for charity, those who practice this self-love see others not as individuals who are lovable in themselves, but as opportunities to feather their own spiritual nests. They mistakenly think they can assure themselves a place in heaven even if they are charitable to others only when God's presence is evident.

While seeing God in others may help us to be more charitable, we need not recognize God in order to have an authentic love for God. How we love God's "little ones" is how we love God. Since God is identified with our neighbors, a true love of them is a true love of God. If we love and appreciate others for who they are, we love and appreciate God for who God is. Our love of God is genuine when we love God, whom we do not always see, by loving those whom we do see everyday.

What is it like to have a love that does not depend upon "seeing God"? It is to live in a world where there are no strangers, no foreigners, no enemies—only brothers and sisters. Should two persons or two peoples quarrel, those with genuine love, the true lovers in this world, do not side with one against the other. They love both persons, both peoples, because they cannot love one brother and hate another. In their love for both, they do what they can to alleviate the suffering that conflict causes. To end the quarrel, they call for forgiveness, reconciliation, and peace. When the fighting of two harms a third, the true lovers show their love for all three by standing with the innocent one whom the other two have injured. On behalf of that third brother or sister, they speak of justice in a loving way to the other two. More radically still, they accept as their own lot the suffering of the poor third brother or sister. Like Christ, who took upon himself the consequences of our sins, true lovers share in the suffering of their brothers and sisters. They suffer with them in the hope that those who perpetrate cruelty and injustice might see the evil of their violence, repent of their destructive ways, and know the love that God has for them.

Contrary to popular opinion, true love is neither a feeling nor an emotion. We do not "fall" in or out of love. Nor is love something we discover, find, or lose. Although strong feelings may accompany it, love is essentially a choice and an act of faith. We decide whether we shall live in or out of love. And when we receive someone else's love, we choose to accept or reject it according to the faith we have in that person. We know from the nature of the commandments of love God gives us that love is a choice fueled by faith and not feelings. If love were basically an emotion, everything would depend on how we felt and God could never command us to love. However, we must choose to love, and this is good news, for it means that there is no waiting to be in love and everything does not have to be perfect before love can happen. The time for love is not next year, next month, or even next week. The time for love is now.

Whether we feel love or not, we are in love the moment we choose to recognize others as individuals, rejoice over their inherent goodness, desire what is good for them, and whatever is in their best interest. Being in love, we do not give or deny our love to others solely on the basis of our feelings or the risk involved. We use the terms "brother" and "sister" to refer to more than just those who look, think, and act as we do. Even when others consider themselves our enemies, our love for God and for them moves us to act with charity and concern, despite our personal feelings. Like the Lord on the Judgment Day, we recognize no restrictions on whom we are to love and accept no excuses for not loving all, especially the poor. Like the just, like the seven Salvadoran doctors and nurses, we may not see God in others. Yet in loving our brothers and sisters as they did, we have a love of God that is worthy of the Kingdom. For life in this world and the next, nothing else is needed. For lovers, nothing less will do.

Epilogue

The day I finished my mission assignment in El Salvador, I flew back to the States, arriving at my parents' home in time to watch the evening news. The stories offered a shocking welcome. Tornadoes had killed ninety-one people. An unidentified gunman had shot and killed a twenty-five-year-old woman as she waited at a bus stop. An elderly woman had died in the blaze from a fire bomb thrown into her home. A man was brought to trial for killing a young woman and wounding two others in the downtown branch of the public library. Shocked by such tragedy and violence at home, I wanted to pick up my bags and catch the next plane back to El Salvador. My family and friends had always worried about my safety in Central America. However, the evening news made me think that perhaps I had been safer in El Salvador than I was in my own hometown. Having lived with disease-carrying mosquitoes, scorpions, bad drinking water, poisonous lizards, and guerrilla warfare, I had learned never to assume for a single moment that I was completely safe. The poor who faced danger daily had taught me that life did not rest in having security; life began and thrived in having faith in God. By their faith, the poor had showed me how to face our many and varied fears, including the fear of death, and overcome them. Inspired by their example, I experienced a new appreciation for life that I hope never to lose. As I watched the TV screen that first night at home, I realized that the best thing I could do for myself in the States was to continue to live by the lessons I had learned in El Salvador.

I am deeply indebted to the poor for what they have taught me about faith. It is true that faith is a gift from God, but it was the poor of El Salvador who unwrapped that gift for me. Indeed, the poor, like us, make mistakes and do not have all the answers but how wondrously God reveals through them what is hidden from the clever and the wise! I know that I have much more to learn from them, but for now I rejoice that we have been given the gift of faith and that we have the poor with us always to teach us how to use it.

May we, by our life of faith, be as good for the poor as they are for us.

Notes

Gifts from the Poor

1. Mark 12:41-44; Luke 21:1-4.
2. Matt. 10:8.

The Child

1. Matt. 18:1-4.
2. Matt. 10:9-10; Mark 6:7-8; Luke 9:1-3.
3. Rom. 8:35-39.
4. Mark 5:1-20; Luke 8:26-39. Also see Matt. 8:28-34.
5. Matt. 2:16-18.
6. Matt. 5:43-48; Luke 6:27-35.
7. Matt. 18:21-22; Luke 17:3-4.
8. Rom. 8:24.
9. Matt. 19:14.

The Lost

1. Luke 15:11-32.
2. Luke 15:23-24.
3. I. Thess. 5:16.
4. Luke 19:10.
5. Mark 1:35-39; Luke 4:42-44.
6. John 8:29.
7. Matt. 28:20.
8. Matt. 6:6.
9. Rom. 14:17.

The Widow

1. Luke 18:1-8.
2. Luke 11:5-8.
3. Mark 14:32-42. Also see Matt. 26:36-46.
4. Luke 11:9-13. Also see Matt. 7:7-11.

The Vigilant

1. Matt. 24:45-51; Luke 12:42-46.
2. Matt. 25:1-13.
3. Mark 13:33.
4. Luke 2:25-38.
5. Luke 3:21-22.
6. Luke 9:18-20.
7. Luke 9:28-29.
8. Luke 12:13-21.
9. Matt. 13:44-46.

The Fisherman

1. Matt. 8:23-27; Mark 4:35-41; Luke 8:22-25.
2. Matt. 14:22-33.
3. Matt. 13:4-23; Mark 4:1-20; Luke 8:4-15.
4. Matt. 14:30.
5. Matt. 4:18-22; Mark 1:16-20; Luke 5:1-11.
6. John 21:1-14.

The Unafraid

1. Matt. 21:23-27; Mark 11:27-33; Luke 20:1-7.
2. Matt. 21:45-46; 26:3-5; Mark 12:12; Luke 20:19; 22:2.
3. Mark 6:14-29.
4. Matt. 14:5.
5. John 19:4-16.
6. Matt. 22:16; Mark 12:14; Luke 20:21.
7. Mark 5:36; Luke 8:50.
8. Matt. 25:14-30; Luke 19:11-27.
9. Matt. 5:13; Luke 14:34-35.
10. Matt. 10:30-31.
11. Matt. 10:28; Luke 12:4.
12. John 14:1.

13. Luke 17:5-6.
14. Luke 22:32.
15. Mark 14:34-42.
16. Mark 4:35-41.
17. 2 Tim. 1:7.

The Called

1. Luke 1:30.
2. Matt. 1:210.
3. Luke 5:10.
4. Luke 12:32.
5. Luke 1:67-79.

The Martyr

1. Luke 24:46-48.
2. Mark 8:35. Also see Matt. 10:39; Luke 9:24; 17:33; and John 12:25.
3. John 20:11-18.
4. Luke 24:13-35.

The Soldier and the Insurgent

1. Matt. 8:5-13; Luke 7:1-10.
2. Luke 23:32-33.
3. Luke 23:39.
4. Matt. 27:44; Mark 15:27.
5. Luke 23:2-5.
6. Luke 23:40-41.
7. Matt. 27:39-43; Mark 15:24-32; Luke 23:35.
8. Matt. 21:31-32.
9. Matt. 24:39-41; Luke 17:30-35.
10. Matt. 7:1-5; Luke 6:36-38.
11. John 18:33-38.
12. Col. 3:11; Gal. 3:28.

13. Mark 7:20-23; John 2:23-25.
14. Matt. 10:17-27; Mark 13:9; John 16:1-4.
15. John 3:16-18.

The Good

1. Matt. 4:1-11; Luke 4:1-13.
2. Luke 23:35-37.
3. Matt. 26:53.
4. Matt. 27:39-43; Mark 15:29-32.
5. Matt. 27:1; Mark 14:64.
6. Matt. 27:24-26; Mark 15:15; Luke 23:24-25; John 19:16.
7. Mark 4:38.
8. John 16:33.

The Poor

1. Matt. 19:38; 16:24; Mark 8:34; Luke 9:23; 14:27.
2. Luke 23:46.
3. Matt. 5:44; Luke 6:35.
4. Luke 23:34.

The Charitable

1. Luke 3:10.
2. Luke 3:11.
3. Luke 3:12-14.
4. Luke 19:1-10.
5. Matt. 19:16-22; Mark 10:17-22; Luke 18:18-23.
6. Luke 13:10-17; 14:1-6; John 5:1-18.
7. Matt. 12:9-14; Mark 3:1-6; Luke 6:6-11.
8. John 9:1-14.
9. Luke 10:29-37.
10. Luke 12:13-21.

11. Thomas Paine, "Agrarian Justice," in *The Complete Works of Thomas Paine,* Vol. I. ed. Philip S. Finer (New York: Citadel Press, 1969), p. 609.

The Lovers

1. July 7, 1980.
2. Matt. 25:31-46.

www.ingramcontent.com/pod-product-compliance
Lightning Source LLC
LaVergne TN
LVHW010550100826
845148LV00013B/2687

* 9 7 8 1 6 1 0 9 7 5 5 6 8 *